Vel

Paris ~ Versai

Velo**SCENIC**
PARIS / LE MONT-SAINT-MICHEL
Cycle through spectacular scenery

EXCELLENT BOOKS
www.excellentbooks.co.uk
01924 609148
First edition printed 2018

ISBN 978-1901464 37 5

Front cover photo:
The greenway at Mont-Saint-Michel © David Darrault – La Véloscénie
Rear cover photo:
River Seine in Paris © R Peace
Frontispiece:
Versailles © R Peace

CONTENTS

ROUTE TOTAL
453.5 KM / 281 MILES (note some figures rounded to nearest half km or mile)

Veloscenic - Paris to Mont-Saint-Michel by Bike

The route

Launched in 2013, France's Veloscenic bike route visits some of the country's most famous sites, linking Notre Dame cathedral in the centre of Paris to the incredible spectacle of the 'Marvel of the West', Mont-Saint-Michel. It takes in no less than four UNESCO World Heritage Sites; as well as the above it links the banks of the Seine in Paris, the sumptuous palace at Versailles and towering Chartres cathedral.

It also threads its way across four French regions, eight départements and three regional natural parks.

At present around 42% of the route is traffic-free and the remainder is very often on minor roads - many so minor as to be virtually traffic-free.

Route surface and signage

The route shown in green on this guide's maps is traffic-free and suitable for new and returning cyclists and families. Veloscenic is signed in its entirety from Paris to Mont-Saint-Michel with the exception of the Massy-Limours-Versailles option (signing due 2018) . The main traffic-free trails are:

Traffic-free Trail Length km / miles	From	To
TGV Atlantic Green Corridor 12km / 7.5 miles	Place de Catalogne, Paris	Massy
Chartres Green Corridor 11km / 7 miles Note: Some road gaps	Near La Villette-St-Prest	Luisant
Condé-sur-Huisne to Alençon 67km / 41.5 miles	Condé-sur-Huisne	Alençon
Domfront to Pontaubault greenway 61km / 38 miles	Domfront	Pontaubault
Mont-Saint-Michel greenway 9km / 5.8 miles (4.5km / 2.8 miles only used by Veloscenic from Beauvoir to Mont-Saint-Michel)	Pontorson	Mont-Saint-Michel

The route logo is usually combined with the 'standard' signage for French cycle routes, a white cyclist on a green background. The number 40 indicates you are also following National Route 40.

Veloscenic has its own dedicated signage, featuring the distinctive circular logo incorporating the Eiffel Tower and Mont-Saint-Michel silhouettes.

You may see signs for temporary sections of Veloscenic in yellow and black, for example around Mortagne-au-Perche where the greenway was blocked by landslip at the time of writing and where you divert onto roads.

How long does it take?

This guide splits the route into ten chapters, each based around a reasonably comfortable day's ride. These are based on distances an average leisure rider would find comfortable. Allow extra riding time for the urban sections as they involve more complex navigation and present a plethora of sightseeing opportunities.

If you want to tackle bigger daily mileages, combining two chapters at a time into a day's riding would give the following five day trip:

Paris > Rambouillet 83.5 km / 52 miles
Rambouillet > Illiers Combray 83.5 km / 51.5 miles
Illiers-Combray > Mortagne-au-Perche 82.5 km / 51 miles
Mortagne-au-Perche > Bagnoles de l'Orne 93 km / 58 miles
Bagnoles de l'Orne > Mont-Saint-Michel 111 km / 68.5 miles

Tackling generally more comfortable daily mileages over the course of seven days could lead to the following mileages:

Paris > Versailles 34 km / 21 miles
Versailles > Chartres 100 km / 66 miles
Chartres > Illiers-Combray 33 km / 20.5 miles
Illiers-Combray > Rémalard 59.5 km / 37 miles
Rémalard > Alençon 63 km / 39 miles
Alençon > Domfront 72.5 km / 45 miles
Domfront > Mont-Saint-Michel 92 km / 57 miles

Further information online

veloscenic.com
This dedicated website has been put together in French and English. There are wonderful, detailed zoomable route maps showing accommodation options and many other services as well as lots of advice on the practicalities of tackling the route. You can also download GPS files for the route for those who navigate electronically.

francevelotourisme.com
A new organisation promoting use of the developing network of long distance cycle routes, and a very useful source of English language information about the route, including maps, stage information and accommodation.

en.normandie-tourisme.fr
Normandy's official tourist website with a good section on cycling in the area.

Practical Information

Cycling with children

Veloscenic is generally easygoing cycling and even when you do pass through hills the gradients tend to be reasonably gentle. It also has a good amount of traffic-free riding, all of which make it well suited to cycling with children.

If cycling with a family, remember to keep children in front of you on roads (or in between if there are two of you), and take special care at road junctions.

What kind of bike?

The best bike to tackle Veloscenic on is a hybrid bike, rather than a racer, due to the small sections with a rough surface. However you can use any bike.

Cycling in France

It is simply a pleasure. France is a cycling nation and accords cyclists status on the road and some great facilities, from wonderful off-road riding to city centre automated bike hire. If you're unfamiliar with cycling in France here are a few handy tips.

You will no doubt know to ride on the right hand side of the road, path or track you are on. However, there is an old rule of the road called priority from the right which is still a consideration. In the absence of all other signs this rule still applies - it means traffic joining from the right has priority - even if on a seemingly minor road. If, though, your road has yellow diamonds on white background signs you have priority, until you come to one with a black line through. Side roads often have stop or give way markings and roundabouts also usually have give way systems so this rule won't apply here. However, this is not always so, and in any case it's wise to make a habit of treating traffic coming from the right with extra caution as some drivers may still adhere to the old law!

In France traffic lights go directly from red to green but do go to amber between green and red. A red light accompanied by an amber flashing arrow pointing to the right means you can turn right as long as you give way to other vehicles. A green light replaced by a flashing yellow light means you may proceed but have to give way to crossing traffic and pedestrians. Where a cycle path is indicated by a white bicycle on a circular blue background, it is obligatory to use it in preference to the road. Where it is on a rectangular background, it is optional.

Bike Hire
For The Veloscenic Route
The following are three reputable and reliable bike hire outlets in Paris and all can offer longer term bike hire for your Veloscenic trip on the assumption you are returning to Paris with the bike. They are also Accueil Vélo accredited (see page 12 for more explanation).

Paris Bike Tour
13 rue Brantome 75003 Paris
01 42 74 22 14   parisbiketour.net

Paris A Vélos c'est sympa
22 rue Alphonse Baudin 75011 Paris
01 48 87 60 01   parisvelosympa.fr

Gepetto et Vélos
59 rue du Cardinal Lemoine 75005 Paris
01 43 54 19 95   gepetto-velos.com

Also in Paris and the Normandy area are:

The Paris Bike Company
29 rue Victor Hugo 92240 Malakoff
09 51 54 59 32   parisbikeco.com

Fontainebleau Bike Rental
They can deliver good quality bikes in Ile-de-France and Eure-et-Loir départements.
06 22 24 43 53 fontainebleaubikerental.com

Loc Vélo
Based in Normandy, they offer a one-way bike rental service all along the Veloscenic route. They can deliver bikes at any point along the route and will pick up the bike from your journey's end at Mont Saint-Michel.
locvelo.fr 06 46 34 37 21

Around Paris
If you don't want to, or can't use your own bike to get around Paris, the city bike share scheme, Vélib, is a great way to get around using a bike for short trips (though not suitable for long term hire along the Veloscenic). Outside of China, it is the largest city bike share scheme in the world and has been running successfully since 2007 and is due to expand outwards into the suburbs. It is a huge undertaking with many thousands of bikes. The City of Paris has appointed a new operator for Vélib for 2018 who will be making electric bikes available for hire for the first time.
velib-metropole.fr/#

A Vélib hire bike passes near Sainte-Chapelle, a stone's throw from the start of the Veloscenic route at Notre-Dame cathedral.

Travel information

Bikes on UK trains (eg getting to London for onward travel to Paris)

Bikes are carried free of charge on most UK trains, but spaces are usually limited and reservations are sometimes required, especially on intercity services. You can reserve a space for your bike when you book or by calling the train operator. There are normally no restrictions on folding bikes. For full UK travel information visit **nationalrail.co.uk** or call 03457 48 49 50

Eurostar

You have three options for taking bikes on Eurostar:
1. Full sized bikes taken on the same train as you. These must be booked in advance (i.e. at the same time as booking your ticket) and cost £30 per bike one way. Allow time before boarding to take it to the baggage office, a little distance from the boarding area at both London St Pancras International and Paris Gare du Nord.
2. As registered luggage, travelling on a separate train to passengers and arriving within 24 hours of the passenger. Bagged bikes of length 85-120cm cost £10 per bike. The cost rises to £25 per bike if the bagged bike is over 120cm long or if fully assembled and not bagged. This service can be booked on the day of travel. Note tandems are not allowed.
3. As hand luggage on the train with you. The bike must be bagged and not more than 85cm in length (in practice this usually means small folders only). Eurostar is at **eurostar.com** or telephone 03448 225 822.

French train operators

French railways (SNCF) will carry, free and as normal luggage, folding bikes or bagged, dismantled bikes to a maximum of 120cm x 90cm.
Many French trains will carry fully assembled bikes, though the number of bike spaces may be limited. This service is generally free of charge but on TGV high-speed trains bike spaces, if available, must be booked in advance. Along Veloscenic you may want to make particular use of trains in and around Paris and express trains are great for getting your bike into and out of central Paris in one short hop:

(RER) (A) RER services are recognisable by an RER logo plus line logo and there are five lines, A to E, operating in the greater Paris area. **ratp.fr/en**

Transilien services run within the Île de France area and, like RER services, carry bikes outside of morning and evening rush hours.
French rail tickets can be booked online from the UK - Rail Europe can give you details of the current system of doing this and can also sell you your train tickets direct.
sncf.com is the website for French trains. www.sncf.co.uk and Rail Europe are now branded as **voyages-sncf.com** and can be telephoned on 0844 8485848.

European Bike Express

This is easy and efficient travel specifically for cyclists. Stops in Northern France include Calais, St-Witz north of Paris (so handy for a UK return after cycling Veloscenic - take RER line D to Survilliers Fosses and St-Witz is about 2.5 km / 1.5 miles from here), Thionville, Nancy, Nemours and Auxerre. Their air conditioned coaches have reclining seats and pull a purpose-built trailer capable of carrying bikes and bike trailers. Runs throughout the summer serving western France on an Atlantic route and central, Alpine and Mediterranean France (and even into Spain) on other routes. Single or return journeys. UK pick-up points down the eastern side of England between North Yorkshire and Kent, with an M62 / M6 feeder service on certain dates.
bike-express.co.uk
3, Newfield Lane, South Cave. HU15 2JW   01430 422111

French local trains offer a 'roll-on roll-off' service

© Joel Damase

Onward Connections

There are myriad options for returning from the end of the Veloscenic route at Mont-Saint-Michel, including a number of ferries or a rail return to Paris and the Eurostar back to the UK. The map opposite shows rail, ferry and signed cycle route links around the area. Main connecting cycle routes for Veloscenic are:

Avenue Verte Paris to London 398km / 247 miles   avenuevertelondonparis.co.uk
Velofrancette La Rochelle to Ouistreham 617km / 384 miles   lavelofrancette.com
D-day Beaches - Mont-Saint-Michel 210 km / 131 miles
dday-montsaintmichel-bybike.com
Tour de Manche Circular route UK / France route using Poole-Cherbourg and Roscoff-Plymouth ferries 1200km / 746 miles   en.tourdemanche.com

There are several return train options back to Paris Montparnasse from Pontorson. Most services use local trains and take around 4 or 5 hours via either Caen, Folligny or Granville. You can connect with the TGV Atlantique high speed service at Rennes which may be a little quicker, though more expensive and your bike will need its own reserved space booked in advance (by contrast bikes can just be wheeled onto many local TER and Corail services).

A special low cost, high-speed service called Ouigo also operates from Rennes to Paris and stops at Paris Massy TGV station which is near the start of the Limours option of Veloscenic - from there you can cycle back up the Veloscenic greenway towards Paris centre. Bikes must be disassembled and packed in a bag no larger than 90cm x 120cm. **ouigo.com**

Another low cost option is Flixbus, which operates directly between Mont-Saint-Michel and Paris and takes over 5 hours. Again, your bike must be disassembled and bagged. **flixbus.com**

Accommodation listings and contacts

The listings in the guide shown with blue numbering ❶ have been chosen as they are near the route, in the main not too highly priced and usually quite near the beginning or end of the day sections. This is just a cross-section of what is available; a little further off the route more accommodation opportunities arise. Veloscenic have a great website at **veloscenic.com** with accommodation and much more. Several national organisations also offer information:

France Velo Tourisme **francevelotourisme.com**

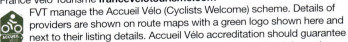

FVT manage the Accueil Vélo (Cyclists Welcome) scheme. Details of providers are shown on route maps with a green logo shown here and next to their listing details. Accueil Vélo accreditation should guarantee secure bike storage and a repair kit. Many also provide cycling information on local cycle routes and a hearty breakfast. We have tried to ensure that all other guide accommodation entries are cycle-friendly but please double check before booking.

FUAJ (French YHA equivalent) **fuaj.org**
Good accommodation section at **freewheelingfrance.com**

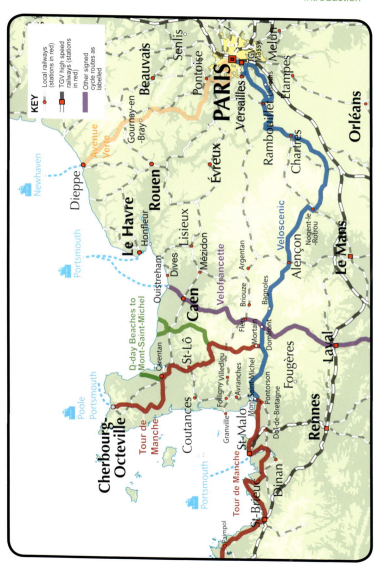

KEY

Local railways (stations in red)

TGV high speed railways (stations in red)

Other signed cycle routes as labelled

Notre Dame cathedral, your route start

© Joel Damase

Paris ~ Versailles

Your start point, the famous 'Wind Rose' outside Notre Dame Cathedral, marks the 'centre' of France - the place all distances are measured from. After threading your way down charming Parisian backstreets you head out along busy rue de Rennes and past the monolithic black tower at Montparnasse train station.

Picking up the Coulée Verte (greenway) leads you southwest, away from motor traffic, to the incredible vistas of the formal gardens at Sceaux. At Massy the route splits, the Versailles option following the charmingly small-scale delights of the Bièvres valley. The smart and compact village of Jouy-en-Josas heralds a long straight approach to Porchefontaine before a grand tree-lined cycle lane brings you to the place d'Armes at Versailles.

Route Info

Distance 34 kilometres / 21 miles
Note: The route splits at Massy, offering a southern route option via Limours that misses out on Versailles but passes through some splendid countryside. Paris-Limours-Rambouillet is 74 km / 46 miles compared to 83.5km / 52 miles for the Paris-Versailles-Rambouillet option. The route to Rambouillet is covered in the next chapter.

Terrain & Route Surface Flat almost all the way. Surfaces on the Coulée Verte range from good quality fine crushed stone to good quality tarmac.

Off-road 68%

Profile

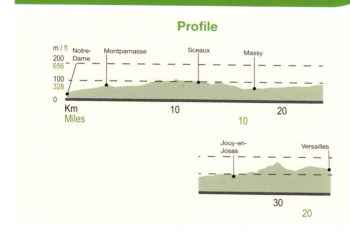

Don't Miss

• Veloscenic's start is at the world famous facade of **Notre Dame Cathedral,** whilst at the other end of the Île-de-la-Cité are **Sainte-Chapelle**, remains of a splendid palace built by early Frankish kings, and the **Conciergerie**, where Marie Antoinette and other leading opponents of the French Revolution were held before meeting their grisly ends.

• Once under way the route passes through the very chic area of **St-Germain** - once bohemian but now rather more upmarket. Premier highlight of the area is probably the **Jardin du Luxembourg**; it was built for Marie de Medici, Henry IV's widow, to remind her of her native Florence. There are grand lawns, flower beds and trees plus an orangerie. Other attractions include sculptures and a pond with nearby cafe. One chief attraction is the magnificent **Fontaine de l'Observatoire**, a fountain with four women representing Africa, Asia. America and Europe holding a celestial sphere above their heads.

North of the Jardin du Luxembourg is the lovely **Saint Sulpice** area, in particular the place Saint Sulpice. For budget eateries try rue Monsieur Le Prince to the north-east of the Jardin. The nearby Odéon-Théâtre de l'Europe was truly groundbreaking when first built in the time of Louis XVI, with a 1900 seat capacity.

• One major attraction just a few minutes away from the start of the route is the **Musée d'Orsay**, one of Paris's most visited sites, housing much famed painting and sculpture dating from 1848-1914.

• Well-known to Parisians but perhaps less well known for visitors is the highly reputable **Le Bon Marché** department store and if you want a real food treat try its **Grande Épicerie.**

• To the east of the route start is the **Quartier Latin**, once a student and bohemian haunt, but these one-time residents have now been replaced by tourists and moneyed residents. There are still quiet, narrow streets around the churches of St-Séverin and St-Julien-le-Pauvre.

Veloscenic in Paris

Versailles

• South of Notre Dame and east of the Jardin du Luxembourg is the area housing the **Panthéon** and the **Sorbonne University.**
The Panthéon was built as a church but now houses the bodies of many of France's great and good; Voltaire, Zola, Marie Curie and Alexandre Dumas to name a few, as well as the remarkable model of Foucault's Pendulum where crowds gather to see the rotation of the earth.
Whilst much of the Sorbonne is private, as you would expect for France's premier university, perhaps the best public spot hereabouts is the **place de la Sorbonne** and the **Chapelle Sainte-Ursule**, which contains Cardinal Richelieu's tomb.
• **Montparnasse** is easily identified by the black mass of its soaring **tower**. Whilst it may not be an architectural favourite of Parisians the view from the top is stunning on a clear day. The nearby **Jardin Atlantique** is built above the train station and is a remarkable construction.

• **Sceaux** is home to the lovely eponymous **château** and its parkland, designed by noted landscape gardener Le Nôtre.
• **Versailles** is world famous for its Louis XIV palace which is one of the most visited monuments in France. Louis was reportedly jealous of his finance minister's château at Vaux-le-Vicomte and so ordered something one hundred times the size. It was once home to the French state administration and a royal retinue of some 3500 noble courtiers.
If you want to glimpse some of the most over-the-top decor in the world the Sun King's home of pomp and pageantry is the place to head for. From 2003 it underwent a **€400 million facelift,** with gardens planted out to the original design and an international search undertaken for original fixtures and fittings.
Some parts require guided visits but not the State Apartments, royal chapel and most famous of all the **Hall of Mirrors**, witness to the post WWI peace settlement.

Paris

Veloscenic

2 **1**

Île de la Cité

i Paris 01 49 52 42 63
parisinfo.com
Gare du Nord Welcome Centre
18 rue de Dunkerque 75010 Paris

Saint-Germain-des-Prés

4
Musée Delacroix
2 **3**

3

4
Gepetto et Vélos

Mabillon

6e Arrondissement

Jardin du Luxembourg

Palais du Luxembourg

Au Point Vélo

0 Metres 100 200 300
0 Yards 100 200 300

Directions (See key for abbreviations)

1 Official Veloscenic start is 'Route Zero', centre of all roads in France, marked by compass outside the facade of Notre Dame cathedral. Wheel your bike across the parvis garden area in front of cathedral, L across Petit-Pont-Cardinal Lustiger, then R along quai Saint-Michel.
2 Head across the place Saint-Michel in front of the impressive fountain-statue and down the street to turn R at place Saint-André-des-Arts onto narrow rue Saint-André-des-Arts. S/O onto rue de Buci, staying on it over rue de Seine.
3 R onto rue de Bourbon le Château and S/O onto rue de L'Abbaye.
4 Pass the church of St-Germain-des-Prés to cross over rue de Rennes. L and L again and R to come back onto rue de Rennes.

Accommodation

To call a French number from the UK add 00 33 at the beginning and delete the first 0 of the French number.

1 BEST WESTERN LE JARDIN DE CLUNY****
9 rue du Sommerard 75005 Paris
01 43 54 22 66   hoteljardindecluny.com/en/

2 HÔTEL DE BUCI****
22 rue de Buci 75006 Paris
01 55 42 74 74   buci-hotel.com

3 ARTUS HÔTEL****
34 rue de Buci 75006 Paris
01 43 29 07 20   artushotel.com

4 LE MADISON****
143 boulevard Saint-Germain 75006 Paris
01 40 51 60 00   hotel-madison.com

5 VILLA DES PRINCES HÔTEL**
19, rue Monsieur le Prince 75006 Paris
01 46 33 31 69   villa-des-princes.com

Bike storage can be tricky in Paris hotels so you might want to consider the following:

HÔTEL DE LA PORTE DORÉE
273 avenue Daumesnil 75012 Paris
01 43 07 56 97   hoteldelaportedoree.com
Around 6km from Notre Dame but have bike storage room in basement. Will store bike boxes whilst you're away and also do bike hire.

BLUE MARBLE TRAVEL
2, rue Dussoubs, 75002 Paris
01 42 36 02 34   Travel company that offers storage of bikes, so possible to leave your bikes here if your hotel will not store them. See following site for detail:
http://bluemarble.org/ParisLuggage.html

🅰 PARIS CAMPSITES
There is one campsite within reach of central Paris, some 10 km (6 miles) from Notre Dame.
CAMPINGS INDIGO PARIS BOIS DE BOULOGNE
2 allée du Bord de l'Eau 75016 Paris
01 45 24 30 00   campingparis.fr
Own tent possible or ready erected tents, gypsy caravans and cottages which can be hired for single nights.

Attractions

✪ Ile de la Cité attractions including NOTRE-DAME, the CONCIERGERIE and SAINTE CHAPELLE (See Don't Miss)

✪ CRYPTE ARCHÉOLOGIQUE
Display of the archeology of the île-de-la-Cité found in the crypt under the square in front of the cathedral.

✪ PLACE SAINT-MICHEL
In the place Saint-Michel the fountain is a mid-nineteenth century construction with dragons spouting water and a statue of the archangel.

✪ ÉGLISE ST-GERMAIN-DES-PRÉS
One of Paris's oldest surviving buildings, dating back to the 10th and 11th centuries.

✪ ÉGLISE ST-SULPICE
Large church fronted by a beautifully elegant square.

✪ MUSÉE DELACROIX
Occupies part of the artist's apartment and workshop.

✪ JARDIN DU LUXEMBOURG
(See Don't Miss)

Veloscenic

Montparnasse

5 At the end of rue de Rennes L down the side of Galeries Lafayette onto rue du Départ. Branch L in front of SNCF station then R onto rue du Commandant René Mouchotte along the side of the station.

6 At R/B place de Catalogne S/O onto the cycle lanes leading onto rue Vercingétorix. You are now in effect on the Coulée Verte traffic-free trail that leads you just about all the way out of Paris.

① HÔTEL VANEAU SAINT-GERMAIN***
86 rue Vanneau 75007 Paris
01 45 48 73 11   vaneausaintgermain.com

② HÔTEL LOUISON***
105 rue de Vaugirard 75006 Paris
01 53 63 25 50   louison.com

③ HÔTEL AIGLON****
232 boulevard Raspail 75014 Paris
01 43 20 82 42   paris-hotel-aiglon.com

④ SOLAR HÔTEL
22 rue Boulard 75014 Paris
01 43 21 08 20   solarhotel.fr

⑤ NOVOTEL PARIS GARE MONTPARNASSE****
17 rue du Cotentin 75015 Paris
01 53 91 23 75   novotel.com

✪ MUSÉE DU GÉNÉRAL LECLERC ET DE LA LIBÉRATION DE PARIS ET DE JEAN MOULIN
Museum honouring this WWII general and the French resistance hero.

✪ MONTPARNASSE TOWER
(See Don't Miss)

✪ JARDIN ATLANTIQUE (See Don't Miss)

Join the Coulée Verte just south of place de Catalogne.

SNCF If you are short of time you can put your bike on one of several trains that head to places further out on the Veloscenic route.

Sceaux & Fontenay-aux-Roses: RER line B2 (destination Robinson) to Sceaux or Fontenay-aux-Roses stations from or Gare du Nord, or Saint-Michel/Notre-Dame stations which Veloscenic passes very shortly after its start.

Massy: RER B4 to Massy-Verrières from Saint-Michel/Notre-Dame station or Gare du Nord.

Versailles: RER C5 to Versailles Rive-Gauche station from Saint-Michel/Notre-Dame station.

Chartres: From Gare Montparnasse. Around 1 hour 10 minutes, direct train.

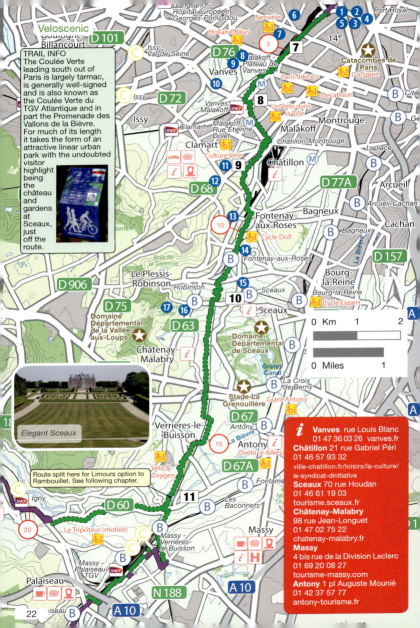

TRAIL INFO
The Coulée Verte leading south out of Paris is largely tarmac, is generally well-signed and is also known as the Coulée Verte du TGV Atlantique and in part the Promenade des Vallons de la Bièvre. For much of its length it takes the form of an attractive linear urban park with the undoubted visitor highlight being the château and gardens at Sceaux, just off the route.

Elegant Sceaux

Route split here for Limours option to Rambouillet. See following chapter.

i **Vanves** rue Louis Blanc
01 47 36 03 26 vanves.fr
Châtillon 21 rue Gabriel Péri
01 46 57 93 32
ville-chatillon.fr/loisirs/la-culture/
le-syndicat-dinitiative
Sceaux 70 rue Houdan
01 46 61 19 03
tourisme.sceaux.fr
Châtenay-Malabry
98 rue Jean-Longuet
01 47 02 75 22
chatenay-malabry.fr
Massy
4 bis rue de la Division Leclerc
01 69 20 08 27
tourisme-massy.com
Antony 1 pl Auguste Mounié
01 42 37 57 77
antony-tourisme.fr

7 At Malakoff Coulée Verte heads across a major road junction past B&B hotel on your R.
8 Just after Malakoff station (yellow M on building) R then immediate L to pass under the rail line. Keep L with the rail line up to your L.
9 At Chatillon Montrouge route bears R across tram tracks at tram stop and into small park.
10 Coulée Verte climbs over small bridge to enter lovely wide linear park area. Pass Sceaux château over to your L **(easy to cycle past!)**.

Take care to pass under next two main roads.
11 Coulée Verte ends at R/B Rond-Point de 19 Mars 1962. R signed Igny alongside D60 (Rambouillet option via Limours straight on - see pages 36-43).
For the Versailles option follow cycle lanes alongside D60 for around 2.6km to R/B on edge of Igny and R at successive R/Bs into Igny Centre. Through centre R onto rue du Dr Schweitzer.

1 LA MAISON MONTPARNASSE**
53 rue Gergovie 75014 Paris
01 45 42 11 39 lamaisonmontparnasse.com

2 ENJOY HOSTEL
5 rue des Plantes 75014 Paris
01 45 40 99 48 enjoyhostel.paris
Dorm beds & private rooms

3 IBIS STYLES PARIS ALÉSIA MONTPARNASSE***
32 rue des Plantes 75014 Paris
01 45 41 41 45 ibis.com

4 IBIS PARIS ALÉSIA MONTPARNASSE***
49 rue des Plantes 75014 Paris
01 53 90 40 00 ibis.com

5 HÔTEL VILLA DU MAINE**
20 rue Ledion 75014 Paris
01 45 42 33 29
villa-maine.montparnassehotelparis.com

6 IBIS PARIS BRANÇION PARC DES EXPOSITIONS 15ÈME***
105 rue Brançion 75015 Paris
01 56 56 62 30 accorhotels.com

7 HÔTEL CLARISSE**
159, boulevard Lefebvre 75015 Paris
01 48 28 18 35 clarisse-paris-hotel.com

8 HÔTEL B&B PARIS MALAKOFF**
2 bd Charles de Gaulle 92240 Malakoff
08 92 78 80 77 hotel-bb.com

9 HÔTEL PATIO BRANÇION
35 rue Edgar Quinet 92240 Malakoff
01 46 56 58 00
le-patio-brancion-hotel-paris.hotel-ds.com

10 IBIS PARIS PORTE DE VANVES***
43 rue Jean Bleuzen 92170 Vanves
01 40 95 80 00 ibis.com

11 HÔTEL B&B PARIS CHÂTILLON **
40 rue de Verdun 92320 Châtillon
08 92 70 25 40 hotel-bb.com

12 IBIS BUDGET CHÂTILLON**
111 avenue de Verdun 92320 Châtillon
08 92 70 12 86 ibisbudget.com

13 HÔTEL LA ROSERAIE ***
32 avenue Jeanne & Maurice Dolivet
92260 Fontenay aux Roses
01 43 50 02 04 hotel-la-roseraie.fr

14 RÉSIDENCE UNIVERSITAIRE LANTERI
7 rue Gentil Bernard 92260 Fontenay-aux-Roses
01 41 13 36 00
www.residence-universitaire-lanteri.com
universityrooms.com Bicycle storage

15 HÔTEL COLBERT***
20 avenue de Camberwell 92330 Sceaux
01 46 60 02 21 hotelsceaux.fr

16 LE CLOS DES PRINCES
60 avenue Jean Jaurès 92290 Châtenay-Malabry
01 46 61 94 49 leclosdesprinces.com/en/

17 B&B LA VILLA DE LA TERRASSE
84, rue Anatole France 92290 Châtenay-Malabry
06 29 68 28 93
facebook.com/villadelaterrasse.chatenay

⭐ CATACOMBES DE PARIS
Older children will love this ghoulish 'attraction'. Bones from charnel houses and cemeteries were stacked up in these old underground quarries.

⭐ DOMAINE DÉPARTEMENTAL DE SCEAUX
(See Don't Miss)

⭐ STADE DE LA GRENOUILLÈRE
Magnificent open air pool open to the public.

⭐ DOMAINE DÉPARTEMENTAL DE LA VALLEE-AUX-LOUPS
Just off the route at Châtenay-Malabry. Landscaped park including 165 species of trees. Chateaubriand, father of French Romanticism lived here.

Veloscenic

12 L at end of rue du Dr Schweitzer . Road becomes track. R under railway and L onto road. Pass Bièvres train station. Jink R then L onto rue des Prés which becomes chemin des Prés de Vauboyen.
13 At Vauboyen station L over train line then R onto bike path to come alongside D117.

14 Split R following cycle lanes then crossing rail lines into Jouy-en-Josas (town centre is back across the rail lines on L). R at R/B onto D446.
15 Follow D446 to split in route by Petit-Jouy-Les-Loges station and R on cycle lanes up D446 (L at split goes to Les-Loges-en-Josas and 'main' route option to Rambouillet).

Versailles accommodation can be very pricey so Buc is often used as a nearby cheaper option.

① CHAMBRE D'HÔTES MAISON DES BOIS
10 chemin de la Butte au Diable 91570 Bièvres
06 74 50 55 63   maisondesbois.fr

② BEST WESTERN PLUS HOTEL PARIS VAL DE BIÈVRE****
1 rue de la Libération 78356 Jouy-en-Josas
01 69 35 43 21   bestwestern.fr

③ CHAMBRE D'HÔTES LES MARRONIERS ***
7 Grande Rue 78350 Les-Loges-en-Josas
01 39 56 65 74   marronniersdesloges.com

④ BUC LOUNGE HÔTEL **
12 rue Louis Massotte 78530 Buc
01 39 56 34 15 / 01 39 56 47 41   bucloungehotel.com

⑤ HÔTEL CAMPANILE VERSAILLES - BUC ***
rue Clément Ader, ZAC du Pré Clos 78530 Buc
01 39 56 26 26 / 01 39 56 26 27
campanile.com

⑥ BEST WESTERN HOTEL VERSAILLES***
avenue Morane Saulnier, 78530 Buc
01 39 56 48 11   thehotel-versailles.fr

⭐ **MUSÉE DE LA TOILE DE JOUY**
Small museum that will be of interest to those with a particular interest in this distinctive floral style decorative technique for fabrics and pottery.

⭐ **MAISON LITTÉRAIRE DE VICTOR HUGO**
The current title for the Château des Roches in Bièvres where the famous romantic writer, Victor Hugo, was a frequent visitor in the nineteenth century. Fine house, park and tearooms.

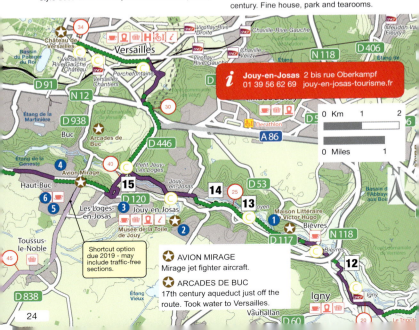

⭐ **AVION MIRAGE**
Mirage jet fighter aircraft.

⭐ **ARCADES DE BUC**
17th century aqueduct just off the route. Took water to Versailles.

ⓘ Jouy-en-Josas 2 bis rue Oberkampf
01 39 56 62 69   jouy-en-josas-tourisme.fr

Shortcut option due 2019 - may include traffic-free sections.

Traffic-free between Bièvres and Jouy-en-Josas

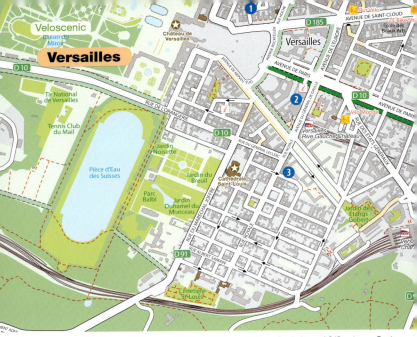

16 Take care crossing the D446 to pass under the main N12 / A86 intersection then cross back over again (Versailles Grand Parc woods to R here) and leave cycle lanes to head into Versailles down rue Rémont.

17 L onto rue Berthelot and S/O onto rue Coste.

18 Pass Porchefontaine station and under rail line then L at main road to follow lovely cycle lanes all the way to Versailles palace entrance.

---

1 HÔTEL LE VERSAILLES ****
7 rue Sainte-Anne 78000 Versailles
01 39 50 64 65 / 01 39 02 37 85
hotel-le-versailles.fr

2 HOTEL IBIS VERSAILLES CHÂTEAU***
4 avenue du Général de Gaulle,
78000 Versailles,
01 39 53 03 30   accorhotels.com

3 ROYAL HÔTEL
23 rue Royale 78000 Versailles
01 39 50 67 31 / 01 39 02 72 09
www.royalhotelversailles.com

4 ▲ CAMPING HUTTOPIA VERSAILLES
31 rue Berthelot 78000 Versailles
01 39 51 23 61 / 01 39 53 68 29
huttopia.com

⭐ CHÂTEAU DE VERSAILLES (See Don't Miss)

⭐ CATHÉDRALE SAINT-LOUIS

Mid-eighteenth century building with impressive paintings, organ and pulpit. At the heart of the lovely old town, the Quartier Saint-Louis, which has many fine old buildings.

⭐ DOMAINE DE MADAME ELISABETH
Park and orangerie, built by Louis XVI's sister.

Paris to Versailles

Viroflay

Versailles

Domaine de
Madame Elisabeth

Porchefontaine

18

17

Huttopia
Versailles

Chapiteau
Méli-Mélo

Stade de
Porchefontaine

Versailles
Grand Parc

16

N

0 Kilometres 0.5

0 Miles 0.5

ℹ **Versailles** 2 bis avenue de Paris
01 39 24 88 88 versailles-tourisme.com
Second office in Versailles at:
1 bis rue du Jeu de Paume
08 92 97 63 05

Passing Chevreuse and Château de la Madeleine on the Veloscenic route

Versailles ~ Rambouillet

From Versailles Veloscenic heads through the lovely Chevreuse Valley passing castles, museums, wash-houses and small picturesque villages such as Châteaufort and Choisel. On small country roads and cycle paths, the route snakes its way through the gentle scenery of the Chevreuse Valley Natural Regional Park. Just off the route, Chevreuse is well worth the short detour. The Château de Breteuil is another very attractive stop-off near the route.

The final run-in to Rambouillet, whose imposing château has hosted many international summits, is through dense forest on a good quality traffic-free forest track.

Route Info

Distance Versailles to Rambouillet 49.5 kilometres / 31 miles

Terrain & Route Surface Easy-going at first but with some stiff climbs between the Chevreuse valley and Cernay-la-Ville. Mainly good quality cycle lanes and minor roads.

Off-road Versailles to Rambouillet 67%

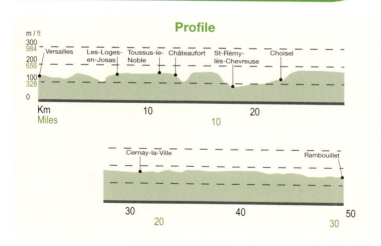

Profile

Chevreuse

Don't Miss

• The **Château de la Madeleine** dominates the town of Chevreuse, the 'honeypot' centre for visitors to the Chevreuse Valley Natural Regional Park, an area rich in historic monuments and lovingly kept countryside which Veloscenic passes through for much of this section.

The château itself is an 11th century castle with stunning views over the Chevreuse valley and free entry. Chevreuse is two minutes cycling off the main Veloscenic route.

• **Château de Breteuil** has the emphasis on family fun at the home of the counts of Breteuil. Tea room open Sundays. Outside attractions include 75 hectares of gardens, a maze and an orangerie whilst inside there are guided tours (French only) and reconstructions of the Charles Perrault fairytales.

• Historic **Rambouillet** is best known for its lovely château but the town is charming in itself and also houses surprises like Rambolitrain, a wonderfully detailed toy train museum.

The château itself developed around a 14th century castle. In 1783, Louis XVI bought the castle and had the estate and neighbouring village remodelled. Later, the château became a residence for French presidents and since the 1940s, it has hosted major international meetings. Children will love the nearby **Espace Rambouillet**, combining plenty of wildlife close up and outdoor activities.

Rambouillet forest has countless oaks and many lakes and attracts over 10 million visitors a year. It is still used for hound hunting today.

Rambouillet

Versailles - Rambouillet Option

Directions (See key for abbreviations)

1 Retrace your route from Versailles to the route split by Petit-Jouy-Les Loges train station. R under railway S Buc and Les Loges-en-Josas. Climb steeply to D120 and R.

2 Pass the church in Les-Loges-en-Josas and head straight on out of village and pick up cycle lanes alongside road.

3 At D938 by Mirage jet R then L by Louis Blériot flying school, using good cycle lanes alongside rue de la Minière (Buc is R, off route, on D938 past impressive aqueduct steeply downhill, and

Châteaufort option L - see below). Road section leads to junction and R onto more cycle lanes. .

4 L onto cycles lanes at D91. Follow these cycle lanes along avenue Léon Blum for two R/Bs then L onto avenue de L'Europe. S/O next R/B and L onto D36.

5 R onto track descending into Forêt Dominiale de Port Royale. Immediate R, S Vallée de la Mérantaise. Cross stream and follow all signs to Magny-Village. L to leave route forestière de Mérancy and climb to Magny church.

6 L and L to D195 and L again S Magny Centre Bourg.

Accommodation

To call a French number from the UK add 00 33 at the beginning and delete the first 0 of the French number.

1 BEST WESTERN THE WISH VERSAILLES
6 bis, rue des Graviers 78280 Guyancourt
01 30 64 04 04 hotelthewish.com

2 IBIS STYLES HOTEL GUYANCOURT VERSAILLES
Place Georges Besse 78280 Guyancourt
01 72 87 99 33 ibis.com

3 MAISON PRAIRIE BONHEUR **
6 chemin des Patissiaux
Le Village 78114 Magny-les-Hameaux
01 30 44 26 08
Large property with 5 B&B rooms and a holiday cottage for 6 people (inc. 3 bedrooms)

4 RÉSIDENCE HÔTELIÈRE VAL HÔTEL
3 place des Dix Toises 78117 Châteaufort
01 39 07 45 50 valhotel.fr

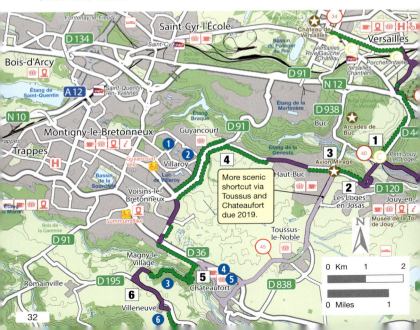

7 R S Villeneuve. First L in Villeneuve. Join cycle lanes alongside D195.
8 R at R/B, S Chemin de la Chapelle. At bend descend **BEWARE STEPS ON STEEP DESCENT.** L onto road, descending to road. S/O rue du Port Royal onto path. Climb to road and L. Cross D906 and follow path over stream past church. Cycle lanes bear R past church alongside road in Saint-Rémy-lès-Chevreuse.
9 Lovely views now across the Chevreuse Valley to the Château de la Madeleine on the hill. You can visit this charming village by staying on the road. Official route heads L onto track chemin rural no. 34. L off track and follow road to split R, S Choisel. S/O junction at Mairie in Choisel to climb steeply. Through La Ferté split L route de la Grange aux Moines.
10 Château de Breteuil on L, main route carries on. At pond by Ferme de la Fillolière R. R onto D40 then R onto D24 following into Cernay-la-Ville. L here onto D906, join cycle lanes.

5 LA MAISON DE LA SOURCE
2 chemin de la Source 78117 Châteaufort
06 15 54 48 44   lamaisondelasource.fr

6 ZENITUDE HÔTEL RÉSIDENCES
50 route de Porte Royal des Champs
78114 Magny-les-Hameaux
01 30 47 89 50
zenitude-hotel-residences.com

7 RÉSIDENCE LES DUCS DE CHEVREUSE
7 route de Choisel
78460 Chevreuse
01 30 07 33 30   lesducs.com

i **Saint-Rémy-lès-Chevreuse** 1 rue Ditte
01 30 52 22 49   saintremyleschevreuse-tourisme.com
Chevreuse 3 rue de l'église
01 30 52 02 27   chevreuse-tourisme.com

Attractions

⭐ FERME DE COUBERTIN
Dairy farm with cows and goats. Sells a range of homemade produce.

⭐ CHÂTEAU DE LA MADELEINE CHEVREUSE
See 'Don't Miss'.

⭐ CHÂTEAU DE BRETEUIL
See 'Don't Miss'.

⭐ FERME DE LA NOUE
Farm produce including pâtés, cheeses and honey

Paris - Limours - Rambouillet option joins here. See pages 36-43 for more detail.

ℹ **Rambouillet:**
1 place de la Libération
78120 Rambouillet
01 34 83 21 21 / 01 34 83 21 31
rambouillet-tourisme.fr

11 After 5.5 km on D906 L onto route du Coin du Bois forest road. S/O D27 S Espace Rambouillet.
12 After 5.3 km on route du Coin du Bois R at track X-roads and follow to lake by Huttopia camping. R to keep lake on your L. Bend L at end of lake.
13 Over X-roads to pass under N10 motorway and S/O onto rue des Aveuses. L onto av Georges Pompidou's cycle lanes.

14 Jink L then R at junction.
15 Route heads L at junction then R through gate into Rambouillet grounds (note shut at 19.30). Quietest bike access to town centre and main entrance to Rambouillet château is through grounds and R (signed) on exiting grounds at Marie Antoinette's dairy.

Paris - Limours - Rambouillet Option

Continued from page 42

26 R off chemin du Mesnil onto route de Sonchamp, alongside pond.
27 L onto rue de Rambouillet (D27), across the centre of the village.
28 Leaving village L onto rue de Paincourt S La Hunière / Greffiers. After around 2.5km on this road R onto track which is route de l'Etang d'Or. This joins the main route at X-roads where you go S/O, to join directions at **12** above.

1 LA MUSARDIÈRE
22 route de Rambouillet
78120 Clairefontaine-en-Yvelines
01 34 84 57 29
tourisme-sud-yvelines.fr/fr/information/34937/
chambres-hotes

2 GÎTE LE FOUR À CHAUX
route de Saint-Rémy-des-Landes
78120 Clairfontaine-en-Yvelines
01 34 84 55 70
lefourachaux78.fr/chambre-vue-potager/

3 MERCURE RAMBOUILLET RELAYS DU CHÂTEAU ****
1 place de la Libération, 78120 Rambouillet
01 34 57 30 00 / 01 30 46 23 91
mercure-rambouillet.com

4 RÉSIDENCE LES VIVIALES
11 rue de la Giroderie 78120 Rambouillet
01 34 57 23 00   giroderie-rambouillet.fr

5 LES CAILLOUX EN VALLÉE DE CHEVREUSE
22 route d'Auffargis 78125 Vielle-Église-en-Yvelines
01 30 41 05 01   chambredhoterobbes.fr

6 CAMPING HUTTOPIA RAMBOUILLET ***
78120 Rambouillet
01 30 41 07 34 / 01 30 41 00 17
huttopia.com

ESPACE RAMBOUILLET
See 'Don't Miss'.

DOMAINE DE RAMBOUILLET
See 'Don't Miss'.

Veloscenic passes through the château grounds

© David Darrault

© David Darrault

Greenway near Gometz

Paris ~ Rambouillet (Limours option)

Whilst this option avoids Versailles by heading south rather than west at the route split near the end of the Atlantic Corridor greenway, it gives you the chance to get more off the beaten track and discover the medieval centre of Rochefort-en-Yvelines as well as the delightful residence of two celebrated writers. The Limours greenway is an oasis of calm that also lets you discover the history of the Aérotrain. (Note: the Paris to Massy section of this chapter is covered in the Paris to Versailles chapter).

Route Info

Distance 74 kilometres / 46 miles

Terrain & Route Surface Some moderate climbs on the road section plus an easy section of traffic-free trail on a crushed stone surface along the Limours greenway.

Off-road 52%

Profile

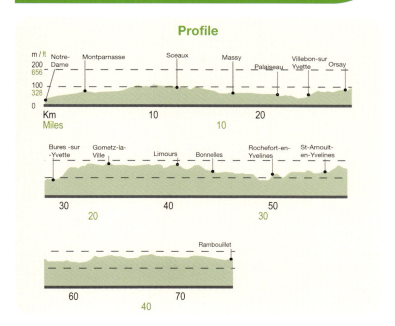

© David Darrault

Château de Saint-Jean de Beauregard

Don't Miss

• Between Limours and Gometz-la-Ville you are cycling in the tracks of history; or rather what might have been history. The **Aérotrain**, created by engineer Jean Bertin in 1964, was a planned future transport system that could reach 300 km/h, moving on a cushion of air. This section of route follows one of the test tracks of the project which was cancelled in 1974.

• The **Moulin de Villeneuve (La Maison Elsa Triolet-Aragon)** at Saint-Arnoult-en-Yvelines was home of 20th-century surrealist writer Louis Aragon and his writer wife Elsa Triolet. On Triolet's death the house and gardens were kept as was and are now open to the public.

• The **Château de Saint-Jean-de-Beauregard** lies just off the route to the south of Gometz. The 17th century grand house is a listed historic monument and the gardens are equally impressive. It also boasts a remarkable structure in the form of one of the largest dovecotes in the whole of France.

• **Rochefort-en-Yvelines** is a gem of a village crammed with ancient buildings and a hilltop church. There is also a ready supply of fine restaurants and accommodation.

Rochefort-en-Yvelines

© Mairie, Rochefort

Directions (See key for abbreviations)

1 At R/B 19 mars 1962 take the exit onto avenue des Martyrs de Soweto. L onto avenue Général de Gaulle along cycle lanes. R on the avenue de Paris towards Palaiseau then R on rue Victor Bash then L on avenue Carnot towards Gare Massy TGV.

2 S/O to bike path in front of RER station Massy-Palaiseau, under the motorway bridge, bearing R. L on bridge to X-rds and S/O onto boulevard de la Grande Ceinture. S/O onto boulevard Diderot. Keep following ahead onto rue Général Ferrié then rue de Paris through the pleasant streets of Palaiseau.

3 Merge with main D988 road, bearing R onto it and at next junction S/O continuing on D988 signed Orsay and Chartres, staying on D988.

4 Keep L where the road splits to stay on avenue du Général LeClerc (the D988 coming into Villebon-sur-Yvette).

5 At main junction in Villebon bear L then R to pick up cycle lanes alongside avenue de Paris, still on D988.

6 Coming into Orsay centre bear R staying on rue de Paris, following to junction by Post Office. R here onto rue Boursier. At main X-rds L onto D446. Follow to R/B and R to rejoin D988 out of Orsay.

7 S/O R/B at Bures staying on D988 signed Gometz and Limours.

8 S/O R/B and into Bures small centre, passing shops. At R/B on edge of Bures L onto rue de Montjay. After 560 m R onto path that starts behind the bench and the bin. Go straight under the tunnel and continue on the Viaduct des Fauvettes.

9 L on path, leaving the forest, and S/O on rue des Rochers. R onto route de Grivery.

10 Pass by cemetery to take bike path in front of it. L at small R/B (3rd exit) and continue on bike path.

11 S/O rue de Janvry (D 131) and cross car park of school Ingénieur Jean Bertin to rejoin bike path.

12 Second exit at R/B to continue bike path by supermarket on edge of Gometz-la-Ville. R onto greenway.

13 At Limours S/O rue de Rambouillet (D24) to continue on greenway.

Accommodation

To call a French number from the UK add 00 33 at the beginning and delete the first 0 of the French number.

1 HOTEL MASSY MERCURE
21, avenue Carnot 91300 Massy
01 69 32 80 20   mercure.com

2 CHOICE HOTELS
2 rue Christophe Colomb 91300 Massy
01 81 91 81 00   choicehotels.fr

3 HOTEL D'ORSAY
2 rue François Leroux, 91400 Orsay
01 64 86 17 47   orsay-hotel.com

4 RÉSIDENCE DES VIGNES
2, rue des Morillons   91940 Gometz-le-Châtel
01 64 86 30 00   hotel-les-vignes.com

5 RELAIS DE LA BENERIE
chemin Vicinal 2 91470 Limours
01 64 91 17 60   www.benerie.com

Attractions

⭐ AÉROTRAIN
See 'Don't Miss'. There are sculptures and paintings of this futuristic project along the way.

⭐ CHÂTEAU DE SAINT-JEAN DE BEAUREGARD
See 'Don't Miss'.

SNCF RER B4 rail line lets you get out of central Paris quickly if you don't want to cycle out of the city and access stations on the Massy-Limours-Rambouillet option. There are stations near the route at Palaisieau, Palaisieau-Villebon, Orsay-Ville and Bures-sur-Yvette. In Paris you can get onto RER B4 at Gare du Nord and Saint-Michel / Notre-Dame. It terminates at Saint-Rémy-lès-Chevreuse.

14 Under bridge and go up on the track on L, just before the gate closing the path.

15 L on bridge onto rue de Malassis. L in Villevert. Stay L on rue de Malassis and rue de Villevert.

16 L at junction and continue on rue de Villevert over bridge.

17 Coming into Bonnelles bear L to stay on rue de Villevert. At R/B R onto D132 S Bullion. Stay on D132 over junction.

18 L onto chemin de Molièr just before bridge and continue onto chemin d'Aumont.

19 Bearing R then L (onto a hiking trail) will take you across the BUSY AND FAST D988 onto road C3 towards La Bâte.

20 Stay R on rue du Lavoir coming into La Bâte. R at T-junction in village and split L to leave village.

21 At junction turn L and come into Longvilliers. S/O X-rds here by Mairie. Bear L out of village onto route du Reculet.

22 TAKE CARE S/O the busy and fast D149 S Reculet and Petit Plessis.

23 Continue on this lovely minor road through Reculet and then through Petit Plessis.

24 Coming into Saint-Arnoult-en-Yvelines R at junction onto rue du Bon Saint-Arnoult. S/O next two junctions following rue de Gâtines and rue Sainte Scariberge. R onto D29 and over bridge. Follow road to R/B at edge of town and R staying on D29 S Clairfontaine.

25 L onto woodland track S chemin du Mesnil.
DIRECTIONS CONTINUED ON PAGE 34

⭐ MAISON TRIOLET - ARAGON
Watermill and residence of famous 20th century writers Elsa Triolet and Louis Aragon at Saint-Arnoult-en-Yvelines. The beautiful mill is now a museum surrounded by a sculpture park.

⭐ ROCHEFORT-EN-YVELINES
See 'Don't Miss'.

① CHAMBRE D'HÔTES LA FOULERIE
57 chemin de la Foulerie 78830 Bullion
01 30 59 58 70   foulerie.fr

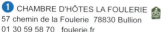

② LE NID DE ROCHEFORT *
34 rue Guy le Rouge
78730 Rochefort-en-Yvelines
01 78 97 02 82 lenidderocherfort.fr

③ AUX HÔTES DE GUY LE ROUGE
73 rue Guy Le Rouge.
78730 Rochefort-en-Yvelines
01 30.41 90 72 / 06 95 15 42 97
auxhotesdeguylerouge.com

④ L'HIBERNIE
7 rue de la Pie 78730 Rochefort-en-Yvelines
01 30 59 55 71   l-hibernie.fr

⑤ LA FERME DE RECULET
11 Hameau de Reculet 78730 Longvilliers
08 90 21 70 70
charme-traditions.com/fr/chambres-d-hotes/org/18982/la-ferme-de-reculet

⑥ AUBERGE DE L'ECUREUIL
89 rue Charles de Gaulle
78730 Saint-Arnoult-en-Yvelines
aubergedelecureuil.fr
01 30 41 20 30

⑦ ⛺ CAMPING CARAVANNING DE LA BOUCAUDERIE
2 rue Stourm 78730 Saint-Arnoult-en-Yvelines
01 30 41 21 29 / 01 30 41 21 29
niconic.free.fr

© Conseil Départemental des Yvelines

Rochefort-en-Yvelines

The river Eure at Chartres

Rambouillet ~ Chartres

Head out of Rambouillet via the château grounds, cross the lovely little Guéville and Drouette valleys then enter the grander Eure valley. Épernon is a fine hilltop town and at Maintenon the arches of the aqueduct border the magnificent castle, where Madame de Maintenon, wife of Louis XIV, lived.

Punctuated by pretty villages, the last section approaches Chartres and its magnificent UNESCO World Heritage listed cathedral, finishing on a greenway with a panoramic entrance to the capital of stained glass and light.

Route Info

Distance 50.5 kilometres / 31 miles

Terrain & Route Surface No really testing climbs but some small but stiff hills up to and around Épernon with an easy run-in to Chartres. Mainly minor roads.

Off-road 10%

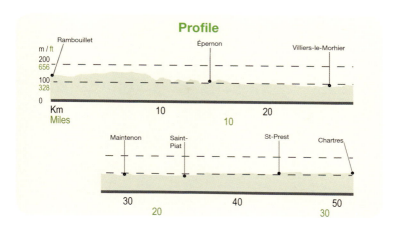

Profile

Don't Miss

• **Épernon** Small, attractive town centre plus the plateau de Diane viewpoint, Prieuré Saint-Thomas with public park and the Conservatoire des Meules et des Pavés, a museum dedicated to stonemasons and pavers.

• The **Château de Maintenon** was built around a 12th century structure but developed into the home of Louis XIV's 'secret' wife Madame de Maintenon, who became second only to Louis himself in terms of France's power politics at the time.

There are fine interiors and wonderfully restored gardens which contain an unfinished aqueduct built with the intention of supplying the fountains at the Palace of Versaillles. The well-known aristocratic line the Noailles inherited the estate and many changes were made in the nineteenth century. The building was severely damaged by allied bombing in WWII but the Raindre family took on the task of its subsequent restoration. From 2005 the Eure-et-Loir General Council took over the running of the estate.

Château de Maintenon

Chartres by the river Eure

• **Chartres** is best known for the two soaring spires of its 13th century cathedral, said to be France's best preserved medieval cathedral, but history almost had it otherwise.

A committee was appointed in the anti-religious fervour of the French revolution to decide on how best to demolish the cathedral. Thankfully it took so long to deliberate that anti-church feeling had time to subside and the cathedral was saved.

In WWII US troops had orders to destroy the cathedral as it was suspected of being used as a lookout but an altruistic US army officer, Colonel Welborn Barton Griffith Jr. volunteered to go behind enemy lines and check if this really was the case.

Again the cathedral was saved as it turned out to be empty.

The cathedral is also well-known for its magnificent 13th century stained glass. The cathedral's huge size compared to the rest of the town is due to the presence of the Sancta Camisia, claimed to be part of the Virgin Mary's robe worn during the birth of Christ.

Other Chartres highlights include the many old bridges across the narrow western channel of the Eure and the flower-lined rue de la Tannerie and rue de la Foulerie on the river's east bank.

47

Directions (See key for abbreviations)

1 Having turned into Rambouillet gardens keep the water on your R. Follow crushed stone path through grounds and exit near Marie-Antoinette's Dairy. Town centre to R here, route L.

2 R onto roadside cycle lanes. L down small road S Guéville. Road becomes a track at 90 degree R. At track end R onto road into Gazeran. L in village at T.

3 R onto C3. Descend over Drouette river.

4 Climb through Émancé then R following D176 signs.

5 In Droue bear R then L onto D122[1] S Épernon.

6 S/O R/B on edge of Épernon and under railway. S/O X-roads and L split by boulangerie. L by town hall. L onto D906. R up rue du Jeu de Paume and L onto rue de la Billardière. Climb to La Vallée Pinault (Hanches). R onto rue Albert Schweitzer then L and S/O next road onto track.

7 Cross tiny bridge - steep concrete ramps here! S/O into forest. Cross further bridge and ascend to road, R here by church at Hanches. S/O onto rue des Granges. Split R down rue des Godets. L onto D101[3] S Villiers-le-Morhier into Ouencé then Ponceaux and on to St-Martin-de-Nigelles, keeping on D101[3].

8 Through Le Coudray and Nigelles, staying on D101[3] into Villiers-le-Morhier. Dogleg L at church (cycle route 41 joins from the R here **DO NOT FOLLOW IT**).

9 L in Rocfoin.

10 R at X-roads S centre. Second L onto av Général de Gaulle (town centre to R here).

11 R at R/B.

Accommodation

To call a French number from the UK add 00 33 at the beginning and delete the first 0 of the French number.

1 LA COUR DU CHÂTEAU
Château de Montlieu 789125 Émancé
06 58 56 86 13   lacourduchateau.com

2 LE COLOMBIER DE HANCHES
8 rue des Bouveteaux 28130 Hanches
06 11 57 29 87   lecolombier-de-hanches.com

3 CHAMBRES D'HÔTES DE L'ECURIE
9 rue du presbytère 28210 Saint Lucien
06 76 89 13 36
www.gites-de-france-eure-et-loir.com

4 B&B LE MOULIN DE LA MALTORNE
Chemin des Bergeries 78125 Mittainville
01 34 94 36 69   facebook.com/Moulin-De-La-Maltorne-697292793750393

5 CHAMBRES D'HÔTES LES CHANDELLES
19 rue des Sablons, Chandelles
28130 Villiers-le-Morhier
02 37 82 71 59   chandelles-golf.com

6 CHEZ GISÈLE ET GÉRARD
2 allée des terrasses 28130 Maintenon
02 37 23 07 72 / 06 08 33 90 13
chambres-dhotes-chez-giselle-et-gerard.business.site

7 AUX CHARMES DE MAINTENON
1 rue du bassin, 28130 Maintenon
07 88 41 63 87
auxcharmesdemaintenon.com/en/

8 CHAMBRES D'HÔTES LE LOGIS DU CHÂTEAU
5 place Aristide Briand 28130 Maintenon
02 37 27 57 32

9 CASTEL MAINTENON ****
1 rue de la Ferté 28130 Maintenon
02 34 40 14 14   castelmaintenon.com

10 ⛺ LES ILOTS DE SAINT-VAL***
28130 Villiers-le-Morhier Chalet hire too
campinglesilotsdestval.com

Attractions

★ MUSÉE DES MEULES ET DES PAVÉS
Museum of stoneworking and quarrying.

★ CHÂTEAU DE MAINTENON
See 'Don't Miss'.

ROUTE V41 VALLÉE DE L'EURE À VÉLO
This route joins Veloscenic at Villiers-le-Morhier. It heads off north-west past Nogent-le-Roi on minor roads then passes Dreux (spur route into town). It joins the Voie Verte de la Vallée de l'Eure to join the D62 south of Bueil. From there, there is a proposed route towards the river Seine.

ℹ **Maintenon**
2 place Aristide Briand
02 34 40 11 95
chateaudemaintenon.fr
maintenon@chartres-tourisme.fr

Veloscenic

12 R onto D19² s St Piat
13 In St Piat pick up D6¹ Keep bearing R out of St Piat to rejoin D19²
14 L at fork at Les Moulins
15 Past Jouy station L rue des Larris
16 Follow D134¹² into La Roche
17 L in St-Prest then leave the D134¹² onto D6. R onto rue Jules Amiot / rue Fontaine Bouillant to join greenway.

18 Cross the river Eure and bear away from it. Bear R past the sign for Abbaye Josaphat.
19 Traffic-free path comes back alongside river and under a railbridge. Head left onto contra-flow cycle lanes along road past sports stadium on R. L under large rail viaduct onto avenue d'Aligre (care required.) This is an interim route; the original route headed L off avenue d'Aligre **NOTE:** Due to be reinstated - see line of route on page 55 and map note.

1 GÎTE DE LA PROVIDENCE
3 bis rue de Berchères 28300 Jouy
02 37 23 94 51 / 06 09 33 08 15
contact@gite-laprovidence.fr
Can accommodate groups up to 35 people

2 LES CHAMBRES DE LA ROGUENETTE
8 rue Détour 28300 Saint Prest
02 37 22 43 22
leschambresdelaroguenette.com
For Chartres centre and south accommodation see pages 52-55 & 59

⭐ FRESQUES DE BEL AIR
Giant murals on modern apartment blocks.

⭐ ANCIENNE ABBAYE DE JOSAPHAT
Benedictine abbey on the pilgrim route to Compostella.

The excellent greenway leading to Chartres

Chartres: From Gare de Montparnasse, Paris. Around 1 hour 10 minutes, direct train.

See overleaf for map location

1 IBIS CHARTRES CENTRE CATHÉDRALE ***
14 place Drouaise 28000 Chartres
02 37 36 06 36   ibishotels.com

2 HÔTEL JEHAN DE BEAUCE ****
19 avenue Jehan de Beauce 28000 Chartres
02 37 21 01 41   jehandebeauce.fr

3 TIM HÔTEL CHARTRES CATHÉDRALE ****
6-8 avenue Jehan de Beauce 28000 Chartres
02 37 21 78 00   timhotel.com

4 MERCURE CHARTRES CATHÉDRALE
3 rue du Général Koenig 28000 Chartres
accorhotels.com

5 HÔTEL BEST WESTERN LE GRAND MONARQUE ****
22 place des Epars 28000 Chartres
02 37 18 15 15   monarque.fr

6 VILLA SAINT-PIERRE
11 place Saint-Pierre 28000 Chartres
02 37 35 07 56 / 06 78 09 76 19
lavillasaintpierre.fr

7 LES CONVIV'HÔTES
10 rue du pot vert 28000 Chartres
02 37 90 88 62 / 06 10 17 17 60
lesconvivhotes.com
B&B with shared kitchen

8 LE PUITS D'OR **
3 rue du Puits d'Or 28000 Chartres
02 37 84 01 01

9 LES CRÉPINIÈRES
23 rue des Crépinières 28000 Chartres
02 37 30 13 33 / 06 07 58 00 09

10 CHAMBRES D'HÔTES DE SERESVILLE
9 rue de l'Arsenal
28300 Mainvilliers
02 37 21 54 70
chambresdhote28.com

11 CAMPING DES BORDS DE L'EURE
9 rue de Launay, 28000 Chartres,
02 37 28 79 43   camping-de-chartres.fr/

Chartres

© Joel Damase

Chartres cathedral and petit train

Veloscenic

Chartres:
8 rue de la poissonnerie
28000 Chartres
02 37 18 26 26
chartres-tourisme.com

Chartres

Parc André Gagnon

Palais de Justice

Jardins de l'Évêché

Centre International du Vitrail

Cathédrale Notre-Dame

Secure bike storage

La Maison du Vélo (hire)

Préfecture d'Eure

Archives départementales

Compa

Église Sainte-Foy

Vélo et Oxygen

Théâtre de Chartres

Les Enfants du Paradis

★ CHARTRES CATHEDRAL
See Don't Miss

★ CENTRE INTERNATIONAL DU VITRAIL
Exhibition of Renaissance stained glass panels with changing exhibitions of stained glass.

★ MAISON DU SAUMON
15th/16th century house now the city tourist office.

★ PORTE GUILLAUME
Picturesque 12th century fortified city gate, largely destroyed by the Germans in WWII. Plans to restore it.

★ RIVER EURE
Bucolic riding along the Veloscenic route, much of it edged by lovely riverside parks.

★ L'ODYSSÉE
One of France's largest swimming and diving centres with aquatic rides and much more.

★ MAISON PICASSIETTE
Built between 1930 and 1962 with broken crockery!

0 Metres   100   200   300

0 Yards   100   200   300

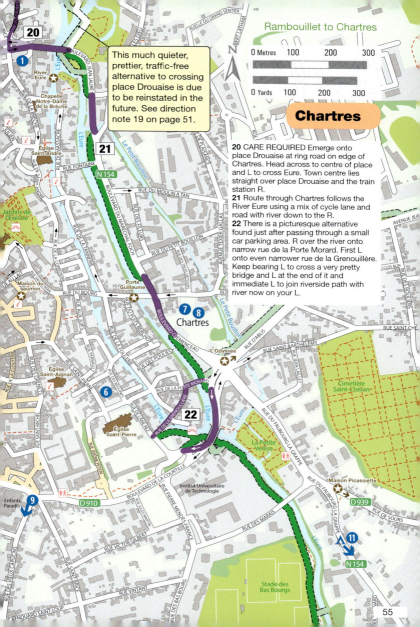

0 Metres   100   200   300

0 Yards   100   200   300

Chartres

20 CARE REQUIRED Emerge onto place Drouaise at ring road on edge of Chartres. Head across to centre of place and L to cross Eure. Town centre lies straight over place Drouaise and the train station R.

21 Route through Chartres follows the River Eure using a mix of cycle lane and road with river down to the R.

22 There is a picturesque alternative found just after passing through a small car parking area. R over the river onto narrow rue de la Porte Morard. First L onto even narrower rue de la Grenouillère. Keep bearing L to cross a very pretty bridge and L at the end of it and immediate L to join riverside path with river now on your L.

This much quieter, prettier, traffic-free alternative to crossing place Drouaise is due to be reinstated in the future. See direction note 19 on page 51.

The church at Illiers-Combray

Chartres ~ Illiers-Combray

After a last glimpse of Chartres cathedral, head in the direction of the emerging valley of the Loir towards Illiers-Combray, crossing the wheatfields of the Beauce plain. Associated with the work of the French writer Marcel Proust, who drew inspiration for his novel "À la recherche du temps perdu" from it, the village of Illiers-Combray is at the heart of the surrounding 'breadbasket' scenery.

Route Info

Distance 33 kilometres / 20.5 miles
Terrain & Route Surface Easy greenway and cycle tracks out of Chartres (some tarmac, others crushed stone) give way to equally easy minor roads.
Off-road 36%

Profile

Central square, Illiers-Combray

Don't Miss

• The **Danse Macabre** found at the Church of Meslay-le-Grenet is one of the best conserved "*danses macabres*" in France. *Danses macabres* were a form of late medieval art depicting death, often personified and dancing along with the living towards their graves. They were meant to reinforce the religious message that no matter how low or high your station in life your fate was the same. To view this example you need to enquire of the *association des amis de Meslay-le-Grenet* on arrival (06 31 12 10 21).

• **Illiers-Combray** was once known simply as Illiers, but added Combray to reflect the fact that

Marcle Proust's famous novel *À la recherche de temps perdu* is partly based on his childhood visits here. Even if you are not a literature fan and don't fancy visiting the Proust museum (his aunt's house), there are many lovely spots in the village. The interior of the church of Saint-Jacques is a wonderfully colourful spectacle, whilst the garden known as Le Pré Catalan, created by Proust's uncle, is an idyllic spot. You can also seek out the wash house of the Romanesque church of St Eman, whose waters are said to be fed by the source of the river Loir (not to be confused with the much larger Loire).

Across the Beauce plain to Illiers

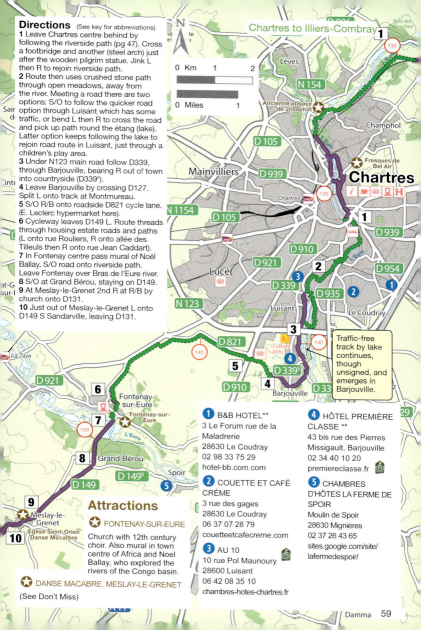

Directions (See key for abbreviations)

1 Leave Chartres centre behind by following the riverside path (pg 47). Cross a footbridge and another (steel arch) just after the wooden pilgrim statue. Jink L then R to rejoin riverside path.

2 Route then uses crushed stone path through open meadows, away from the river. Meeting a road there are two options: S/O to follow the quicker road option through Luisant which has some traffic, or bend L then R to cross the road and pick up path round the étang (lake). Latter option keeps following the lake to rejoin road route in Luisant, just through a children's play area.

3 Under N123 main road follow D339, through Barjouville, bearing R out of town into countryside (D339⁹).

4 Leave Barjouville by crossing D127. Split L onto track at Montmureau.

5 S/O R/B onto roadside D821 cycle lane. (E. Leclerc hypermarket here).

6 Cycleway leaves D149 L. Route threads through housing estate roads and paths (L onto rue Rouliers, R onto allée des Tilleuls then R onto rue Jean Caddart).

7 In Fontenay centre pass mural of Noël Ballay, S/O road onto riverside path. Leave Fontenay over Bras de l'Eure river.

8 S/O at Grand Bérou, staying on D149.

9 At Meslay-le-Grenet 2nd R at R/B by church onto D131.

10 Just out of Meslay-le-Grenet L onto D149 S Sandarville, leaving D131.

Traffic-free track by lake continues, though unsigned, and emerges in Barjouville.

Attractions

⭐ FONTENAY-SUR-EURE

Church with 12th century choir. Also mural in town centre of Africa and Noel Ballay, who explored the rivers of the Congo basin.

⭐ DANSE MACABRE, MESLAY-LE-GRENET

(See Don't Miss)

① B&B HOTEL**
3 Le Forum rue de la Maladrerie
28630 Le Coudray
02 98 33 75 29
hotel-bb.com.com

② COUETTE ET CAFÉ CRÈME
3 rue des gages
28630 Le Coudray
06 37 07 28 79
couetteetcafecreme.com

③ AU 10
10 rue Pol Maunoury
28600 Luisant
06 42 08 35 10
chambres-hotes-chartres.fr

④ HÔTEL PREMIÈRE CLASSE **
43 bis rue des Pierres
Missigault, Barjouville
02 34 40 10 20
premiereclasse.fr

⑤ CHAMBRES D'HÔTES LA FERME DE SPOIR
Moulin de Spoir
28630 Mignières
02 37 26 43 65
sites.google.com/site/lafermedespoir/

11 Bend L at this junction (ignoring D149 R to Nogent-sur-Eure). Keep on D149 into and through Blandainville, ignoring many minor turnings.
12 R onto D108 at X-roads, leaving Blandainville. L by Virgin Mary statue S Petit Chasny on D108

13 L, leaving road hamlet Beaurouvre, onto sandy track skirting medical centre.
14 Meet D921, L onto wide crushed stone path.
15 S/O R/B coming into Illiers-Combray, leaving cycle lanes but staying on D921.

Accommodation

To call a French number from the UK add 00 33 at the beginning and delete the first 0 of the French number.

1 CHAMBRES D'HÔTES ETAPE ZEN
32 rue de Chartres 28120 Illiers-Combray
02 35 82 16 52
etapezen.fr

2 HÔTEL DE L'IMAGE **
18 place de l'Église 28120 Illiers-Combray
02 37 24 02 83 / 07 83 54 06 64 / 09 56 82 42 00
hotel-eure-loir-proust-illiers.fr

3 LOGIS HÔTEL LES AUBÉPINES ***
17 avenue Georges Clemenceau
28120 Illiers Combray
02 37 24 49 49
hotel-lesaubepines.com

4 CAMPING LE BOIS FLEURI ***
route de Brou 28120 Illiers-Combray
camping-chartres.com

 ILLIERS-COMBRAY

(See Don't Miss)

Veloscenic south of Chartres

© Joel Damase

Illiers-Combray: From Gare de Montparnasse, Paris. Around 1 hour 40 minutes to 2 hours, changing at Chartres. Local trains (TER) with free bike spaces.

Thiron-Gardais abbey towers over a bakery

Illiers-Combray ~ Nogent-le-Rotrou

The route leaves the Beauce wheatfields to enter the Perche Regional Park. Lush green country landscapes, rolling hills, villages, manors and the possibility of coming across the strong and sturdy draught horse and symbol of the region, the Percheron await. The wonderfully quirky Frazé château and the ancient abbey at the heart of attractive Thiron-Gardais are visual and historic highlights.

Veloscenic takes in small roads over the foothills of the Perche - which sometimes require some effort, but splendid views are the reward. This section's end takes you in front of Saint-Jean Castle coming into Nogent-le-Rotrou, the historical capital of the Perche counts.

Route Info

Distance 44 kilometres / 27 miles

Terrain & Route Surface Hilly minor roads as you enter the Perche Regional Natural Park.

Off-road 1%

Profile

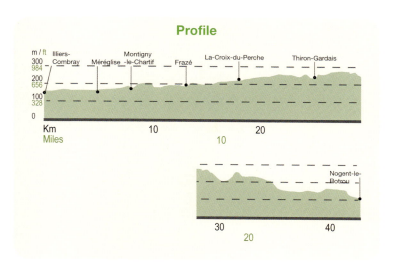

Don't Miss

• Frazé Castle and Gardens
It feels like you get several castles in one at Frazé. The original was totally destroyed during the Hundred Years War and replaced in the 15th century and vestiges of this are still visible, for example in the tower of Saint-François. In the 16th century a Renaissance building was added, and in the 17th and 18th centuries more new buildings erected.

The complex was renovated in the 19th century, then in the first half of the 20th century the park and French gardens added.

• Thiron-Gardais Abbey has a venerable history, being the home of the 'grey' monks who had a strict religious code and emphasis on manual labour. Their Tironensiam order spread from its base here as far as Scotland and Ireland. Impressive interior and gardens.

Frazé castle

Château Saint-Jean at Nogent

• The main sight in **Nogent-le-Rotrou** is undoubtedly the ancient castle with a particularly impressive ancient dungeon. Today the castle houses a museum about the Perche region that surrounds it.

Other attractions in Nogent include Saint Jean Marches, a long series of 16th century steps. Around the bottom of the steps and along rue du Paty are some impressive ancient buildings. The 16th century Maison du Bailli on rue Saint-Laurent stands out. The Church of Saint-Laurent dates from the 16th century and contains a well-known *mise au tombeau* (burial of Christ sculpture).

Directions (See key for abbreviations)

1 From Illiers-Combray market place L onto rue du Docteur Proust. S/O over small square onto rue du Chêne Doré. R and R again onto promenade de la Fontaine. Bend L over footbridge and S/O (Pré Catalan garden signed to R here). R at road. L then R at next two T-junctions.

2 S/O D921. Cross rail tracks and through La Patrière. R at tiny X-rd and L at more main road.
3 L at T junction coming into Méréglise and straight through centre.
4 In Montigny-le-Chartif S/O in front of château, S Brou and Frazé.

Accommodation

To call a French number from the UK add 00 33 at the beginning and delete the first 0 of the French number.

⭐ See overleaf for attractions.

1 CHAMBRES D'HÔTES LA BELLE MORINIÈRE
5 La Morinière 28160 Frazé
09 81 74 13 05   labellemoriniere.com

> **SAINT-JACQUES BY BIKE / LOIR BY BIKE**
> Much of the Veloscenic route from Villiers-le-Morhier to Illiers-Combray is on the Saint-Jacques cycling route, but at Illiers the Saint-Jacques route leaves Veloscenic and heads south through Châteaudun and Vendôme. About 20km from Vendôme it meets the Vallée du Loir cycle route; head off east through rolling countryside towards Angers (the last section is unsigned but there is a carnet map book available). At Angers you can join the mighty Loire à Vélo route which stretches from the Atlantic coast to Burgundy.
>
>

Ancient abbey at Thiron-Gardais

1 L'ÉTAPE DES SAVEURS
6-8 rue du 8 mai 1945
28160 Frazé
02 37 29 06 20   letape-des-saveurs.com
Restaurant & B&B

2 AUBERGE DE L'ABBAYE ***
15 rue du commerce 28480 Thiron-Gardais
02 37 37 04 04   aubergedelabbaye.fr
Hotel-restaurant

Attractions

⭐ MÉRÉGLISE
Featuring 13th century statues *Les Trois Maries.*

⭐ MONTIGNY-LE-CHARTIF
Attractive church and lavoir.

⭐ CHÂTEAU DE FRAZÉ
(See Don't Miss)

⭐ ABBAYE DE THIRON-GARDAIS
(See Don't Miss for Abbey). Small attractive town
with nice range of shops and the Royal Military
College has a museum and gardens.

⭐ ÉGLISE ST MARTIN
Incredible painted wooden ceiling.

⭐ NOGENT-LE-ROTROU
See 'Don't Miss' and overleaf.

5 Entering Frazé L and cross river Foussarde. At
X-roads R and pass château.
6 L on D110 S Nogent-le-Rotrou just out of Frazé.
7 Split L in La-Croix-du-Perche on D110.
8 R onto D110⁶ S Gardais.
9 In forest area head L for Les Bois Aux Clercs

10 R at housing estate coming into Thiron-Gardais.
Split L then R down ruelle de la Motte then across
high street (centre down to L) to pass Abbey. Road
doubles back L towards main street. R onto rue de
Fossés (**small alley - easy to miss**).
R and R again onto D368⁸.

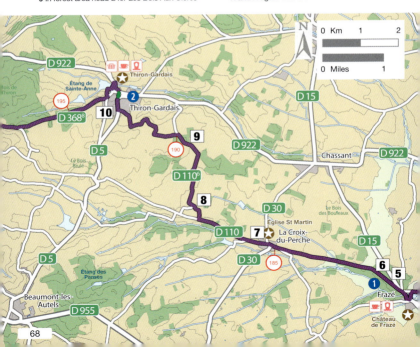

Illiers-Combray to Nogent-le-Rotrou

11 L in La Gaudine onto D110 and R onto D368[8] S Le Goulet.

12 Immediate R at X-roads in Le Goulet onto D368.

13 L S Champeaux and Les Pottiers. R at T-junction.

14 S/O at X-roads onto D112[1]. Stay on it at next junction.

15 R at T-junction onto D112 and into Nogent. Third exit at next R/B.

---

3 MANOIR DU BOIS JOLY - GÎTE DU FOURNIL
28400 Margon
02 37 52 64 86 / 06 89 58 28 74
facebook.com/manoirduboisjoly
Gite is only bookable by the week but there is also a gypsy style caravan bookable for single nights.

4 ⛺ CAMPING LE BOIS JAHAN ***
Le Bois Jahan 28400 Brunelles
02 37 52 14 73 / 06 45 30 66 85 / 02 37 52 14 73
leboisjahan.com

Nogent-le-Rotrou

Veloscenic

1 CHAMBRES SAINT-JEAN 🏠
24 Rue Saint-Jean
28400 Nogent le Rotrou
02 37 52 92 25 / 06 75 67 79 54
chambres-dhotes-saint-jean.business.site

2 AU LION D'OR ** 🏠
28 place Saint-Pol 28400 Nogent le Rotrou
02 37 52 01 60
hotelauliondor.fr

3 HÔTEL SULLY *** 🏠
Le Clos Couronnet 28400 Nogent le Rotrou
02 37 52 15 14 / 02 37 52 15 20
hotelsullynogent.fr

4 LE 42 🏠
42 Rue Saint-Hilaire 28400 Nogent-le-Rotrou
06 87 02 28 18
le-42-chambres-dhotes.business.site

5 BRIT HOTEL – HÔTEL DU PERCHE ***
rue de la Bruyère 28400 Nogent-le-Rotrou
02 37 53 43 60   brithotel.com

6 ⛺ CAMPING MUNICIPAL DES VIENNES
rue des Viennes 28400 Nogent-le-Rotrou
02 37 52 80 51   ville-nogent-le-rotrou.fr

---

16 Follow rue St Jean to castle entrance. Route turns R here up rue du Château.
17 Cross car park at place Sully and L downhill.

18 R at major junction onto main street. Route now exits town by going L down rue St Hilaire at next junction then immediate R over river by the church and after a short while joining rue Sainte-Anne.

⭐ **CHÂTEAU MUSÉE SAINT JEAN**
The counts of Perche lived in the castle until the beginning of the 12th century, the era of terrifying Norman raids. In 1428, during the Hundred Years War, the castle was taken by the English and burned, but the massive donjon remained, though abandoned.
Subsequent cycles of war and restoration mean the castle in its present form is a municipal museum of local Percheron history as well as hosting local exhibitions and events.

⭐ **L'ÉGLISE SAINTE HILAIRE**
15th and 16th century church.

⭐ **L'ÉGLISE NOTRE DAME**
Originally a refuge for pilgrims heading to Santiago de Compostella. Now it houses a famous collection of nativity statues.

⭐ **AQUAVAL**
Indoor, outdoor and diving pools plus tenpin bowling alley. Open daily.

SNCF Some direct trains from Paris Montparnasse to Nogent-le-Rotrou, or you may have to change at Chartres or Le Mans (the latter if using the TGV service out of Paris which costs twice as much as the local service). The service takes around two hours and also links with Chartres.

Rolling Perche countryside

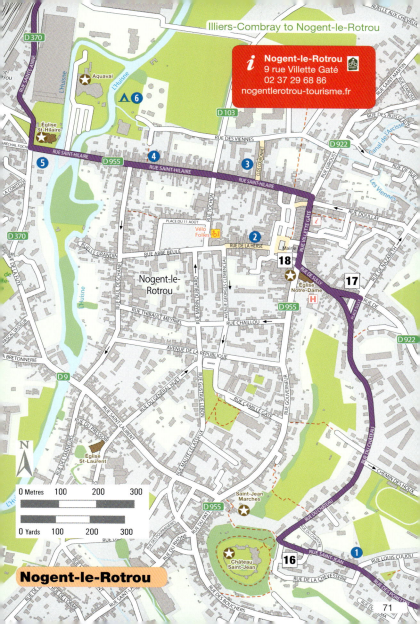

Nogent-le-Rotrou
9 rue Villette Gaté
02 37 29 68 86
nogentlerotrou-tourisme.fr

D 370

RUE SAINTE-ANNE

Aquaval

L'Huisne

△ 6

D 103

Église
St-Hilaire

RUE DES RUISSEAUX

RUE SAINT-MARTIN

RUE DES VIENNES

MARÉCHAL FOCH

RUE SAINT-HILAIRE

D 955

5

4

RUE SAINT-HILAIRE

COEUR COURONNÉ

3

RUE SAINT-HILAIRE

D 922

RUE GIROUST

Les Viennes

LA COMTESSE

RUE FOCHON

RUE DOUILLAY

D 370

PLACE DU 11 AOÛT

Vélo Folies

RUE ABBÉ BEULÉ

RUELLE GRANDIN

RUE PAUL DESCHANEL

Nogent-le-Rotrou

RUE DE LA HERSE

2

Mairie

18

RUE VILLETTE GATÉ

i

RUE DE SULLY

Église
Notre-Dame

17

RUE DE NAZARETH

L'Huisne

RUE MARIN DUBUARD

RUE GEORGES CLEMENCEAU

H

D 955

RUE THIBAULT MEYNIEL

RUE CHAILLOU

RUE DE

PASCAL VASSEUR

BRETONNERIE

AVENUE DE LA RÉPUBLIQUE

D 9

RUE DU GÉNÉRAL HUET

RUE GUSTAVE LEBON

RUE CAMILLE GATÉ

RUE GOUVERNEUR

D 922

RUE SAINT-LAURENT

RUE DU PRESSOIR

RUE DES TANNEURS

Église
St-Laurent

RUE MAURICE GLASGOW

RUE DU CHÂTEAU

CHEMIN DES HOUX

N

0 Metres 100 200 300

0 Yards 100 200 300

Saint-Jean
Marches

RUE DE LA LÉCOMETTE

D 955

RUE DU PÂTY

RUE DU RHÔNE

Château
Saint-Jean

16

RUE DU CHÂTEAU

RUE SAINT-JEAN

1

RUE LOUIS CULIOLI

RUE DES FORÊTS

RUE DE LA CHEVESSERIE

RUE DES BOUCHERS

Nogent-le-Rotrou

On the greenway out of Nogent

Nogent-le-Rotrou ~ Mortagne-au-Perche

On this section you will roll easily along long sections of greenway, through the wonderful landscapes of the old Perche province, taking in villages, mills and manors. Rémalard and Mortagne-au-Perche are both fine towns with many lovely tranquil corners to explore.

Route Info

Distance 38.5 kilometres / 24 miles

Terrain & Route Surface Some climbing out of Nogent, then onto the former rail line, now a traffic-free trail, which has an unsealed but very well-compacted surface.

Off-road 81%

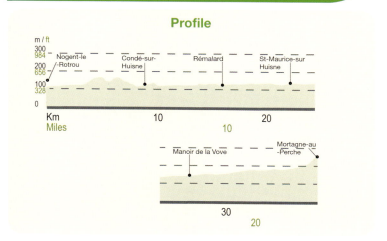

Profile

m / ft

300 / 984
200 / 656
100 / 328
0

Nogent-le-Rotrou   Condé-sur-Huisne   Rémalard   St-Maurice-sur-Huisne

Km
Miles

10

20

10

Manoir de la Vove   Mortagne-au-Perche

30

20

Statue of Alain, Mortagne

73

Don't Miss

• The Perche region once counted up to 400 mansions similar to the **Manoir de la Vove**.
Today, there are about a hundred of them, most of them privately owned. Manoir de la Vove though is open Saturday and Monday afternoons and lets you experience something of the atmosphere of the Hundred Years War, when French and English armies battled for advantage across much of Northern France.

Though initially part defensive fortification and part house, after the end of the Hundred Years War many Manoirs were renovated by nobles to provide themselves with prestigious homes.
• **Villeray** is an idyllic hamlet on the Huisne river, perched over its banks. Its small houses climb up a narrow slope and are fine examples of traditional Percheron buildings. It has been a classified site since 1975.

Typical Perche architecture and countryside

Eating out in place du Général de Gaulle in Mortagne-au-Perche

• **Mortagne-au-Perche** is only a small town but can claim the title of historic capital of the county of Le Perche.

Place du Général de Gaulle is the attractive, busy hub of the town and unusually features a corn exchange. It's also a great eating spot with plenty of pavement cafes and restaurants. There are also ancient narrow paved streets, the Gothic-style Notre-Dame church, a lovely town hall (great views from the garden behind it) and the *Maison des Comtes du Perche*, which includes the Musée Alain. The museum celebrates philosopher Emile-Auguste Chartier, known as Alain, who was born in Mortagne. The old town found to the east of Notre-Dame church is especially quiet and attractive and houses the Crypte Saint-André.

The third weekend in March, the village speciality – black pudding – is honoured during a well-known festival, the Foire au Boudin de Mortagne.

Sundials are also a real local curiosity - no fewer than 27 have been catalogued around the town.

Veloscenic

D 11

D 10

L'Huisne

Rémalard

Moto culture loisirs

Rémalard

5

3 **4**

4

230

Bellou-sur-Huisne

D 920

L'Âne Perché
Dorceau

D 10

L'Huisne

D 11

225

Verrières

Saint-Germain-des-Grois

Villeray
Spa Pom

2

6 D 203

Condeau

D 10

3

SNCF

Condé-sur-Huisne

1

Condé-sur-Huisne

La Ballastière

220

Mélrose Cabaret

2

L'Huisne

Dancé

Saint-Pierre-la-Bruyère

D 623

D 918

D 923

Berd'huis

215

Margon

D 955

D 923

1

D 955

Nogent-le-Rotrou

SNCF

212

D 9

Nogent-le-Rotrou

H **i**

Nogent-le-Rotrou

D 922

Champro
Perch

Saint-Hilaire-sur-Erre

L'Huisne

Erre

D 923

D 955

D 112

D 923

N

0 Km 1 2

0 Miles 1

Directions (See key for abbreviations)

1 Follow rue Sainte-Anne out of Nogent to bend L then R over the railway, following the rail line on your R now.

2 Climb through wood on D623 then descend to Condeau, going R by the church.

3 At X-roads Condé-sur-Huisne is R on official route (greenway on L just entering village) but you can shortcut by going S/O, splitting R S La Haute Roche and meeting the greenway to go L onto it.

4 Rémalard's neat town centre just up to the R here off the greenway. Signage to other villages off the greenway is also generally good.

Accommodation

To call a French number from the UK add 00 33 at the beginning and delete the first 0 of the French number.

① CHAMBRES D'HÔTES LE MUSSET
rue Du 8 Mai 1945, 61110 Condé-sur-Huisne
02 33 73 70 31

② HOTEL-SPA RESTAURANT DOMAINE DE VILLERAY   Villeray   61110 Condeau
02 33 73 30 22   domainedevilleray.com

③ LE CHÊNE REMALARD
28 rue de Monthue 61110 Rémalard
02 33 25 71 39   gites-de-france.com

④ HÔTEL COTÉ PARC
11 – 13 place du Général de Gaulle
61110 Rémalard   02 33 83 02 51   cote-parc.fr

⑤ ⛺ CAMPING DES BORDS DE L'HUISNE **
2 rue de l'Huisne 61110 Rémalard
02 33 73 71 23
remalardenperche.fr/vie-de-la-commune/camping/

⑥ GÎTE 1 RUE DU PONT DE L'HUISNE
61110 Sablons-sur-Huisne
02 33 28 07 00   gites-de-france-orne.com

Attractions

⭐ MELROSE CABARET

Variety of song and dance shows at Condé-sur-Huisne. Dining available with the show.

⭐ SPA POM AT DOMAINE DE VILLERAY

Sumptuous sounding health treatments at this hotel, open to non-residents too. For the village itself see Don't Miss.

⭐ L'ÂNE PERCHÉ

Donkey rides along the greenway and quiet roads of the Perche.

SNCF Trains from Paris Montparnasse to Condé-sur-Huisne, changing at Chartres, Nogent-le-Rotrou or Courville-sur-Eure. The journey takes around two hours.

© Joel Damase

Traffic-free at Boissy-Maugis

➊ LE BISTROT DES ÉCURIES
La Grande Maison 61110 Boissy-Maugis
02 33 25 46 06
bistrot-des-ecuries.com

✪ RÉMALARD
Small attactive town centre with plenty of attractive shops. Also in the town is La Petite Rochelle, themed gardens open in summer only.

✪ MANOIR DE LA VOVE
Group visits by appointment only but a short hop from the trail and visible from it. Ancient, impressive manor house typical of the area.

✪ FERME DE L'ABSOUDIÈRE
Guided countryside rides in a horse-drawn carriage using the impressive Percheron horses that have been the workhorses of the area.

Bastille Day celebrations, Rémalard

En route near the Manoir de la Vove

© Joel Damase

Mortagne-au-Perche

© David Darrault

Mortagne-au-Perche
36 place du Général de Gaulle
02 33 83 34 37
ot-mortagneauperche.fr

5 Greenway blocked at time of writing. Follow yellow deviation signs on meeting the road here. The road climbs towards a water tower and at the first junction immediate R. Follow minor roads, passing La Bourdonnière and La Reinière farmsteads to emerge at a R/B. Second R here and follow D938 which leads to Mortagne centre, crossing the trail on your way, by a restaurant housed on the old station.
Access the trail again by going past the Restaurant du Gare.

1 JARDIN DE LA BOURDONNIÈRE
61400 Réveillon
02 33 25 04 19
bourdonniere.free.fr/chambresdhotes.html
B&B set in 5 acres of gardens

2 CHAMBRE D'HÔTES MAISON DU SABOTIER/LE PARI FOU
Le Bignon 61400 Saint-Denis-sur-Huisne
02 33 73 13 02   gites-de-france-orne.com

3 HÔTEL LE TRIBUNAL ***
4, place du Palais 61400 Mortagne-au-Perche
02 33 25 04 77   hotel-tribunal.fr

4 HÔTEL DES TAILLES
9 rue des Tailles 61400 Mortagne-au-Perche
06 16 90 32 51 / 02 50 47 95 36
hotelleriedestailles.com

5 CHAMBRES D'HÔTES LA PORTE ROUGE
4 rue du Mail 61400 Mortagne-au-Perche
02 33 25 39 95   laporterouge.fr
Vegetarian B&B with homegrown produce

6 CHAMBRES D'HÔTES LE CYTISE
20 rue des Vents 61400 Mortagne-au-Perche
02 33 25 05 41

7 HÔTEL RESTAURANT GENTY HOME
4 rue Notre Dame 61400 Mortagne-au-Perche
02 33 25 11 53   hotel-restaurant-soiree-etape.fr

8 LA FERME DU GROS CHÊNE
61400 Mortagne-au-Perche
02 33 25 02 72 / 06 30 69 53 42
fermedugroschene.com

⭐ CRAZY GOLF AT MAUVES-SUR-HUISNE
Charming mini-golf.

⭐ LA MAISON FERRÉ
Experts in all kinds of cider production found right by the trail at Comblot. Naturally you can taste and buy the wares.

⭐ JARDIN DE LA BOURDONNIÈRE
Five acre garden

⭐ MORTAGNE-AU-PERCHE
See Don't Miss. Also the town has a swimming pool, La Galerie (exhibitions of individual artists), a cinema that includes a museum of cinema, an arts centre and a racecourse with beautiful listed stands.

Mortagne-au-Perche

© David Darrault

Veloscenic

Alençon's imposing centre

Mortagne-au-Perche ~ Alençon

Continue along the greenway and the rolling countryside of the Perche before entering the Normandy-Maine Regional Park. On the way, Le Mêle-sur-Sarthe is an attractive stop-off, with its lake and recreation complex.

The greenway then goes through the lush forest of Bourse and joins a series of small roads through hamlets before reaching the magnificent centre of Alençon. The capital of the Orne founded its reputation on Alençon needle lace and these days is a bustling town with some wonderful buildings.

Route Info

Distance 40 kilometres / 25 miles

Terrain & Route Surface Largely unsealed greenway before a small road section at Valframbert then good quality urban cycle paths and town centre roads into Alençon.

Off-road 88%

Profile

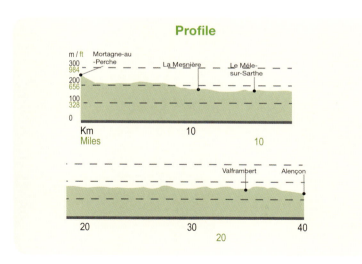

Don't Miss

• **Le Mêle-sur-Sarthe** is an attractive little town with a large leisure lake that allows free swimming and has plenty of leisure and child-friendly activities (generally open weekends in May, June and September, and daily in July and August).

Traffic-free near Le Mêle-sur-Sarthe

Attractive Alençon

• **Alençon** was famous in the 17th century for its fine lacework decorated with miniature flowers (*point d'Alençon*) and whilst the industry has died out there is a museum dedicated to its history with a workshop where the lace is still handmade. It's a painstaking job with twenty hours work required to produce a piece the size of a postage stamp.

Other town attractions include the church of Notre-Dame with its fine stained glass and the Martin family house, which was the birthplace of Saint Thérèse of Lisieux. The Château des Ducs is close to the lacemaking museum and though it looks imposing it's not open to the public.

There are several attractive pedestrianised streets for shopping and cafe-sitting here too plus attractive buildings like the town hall and the corn exchange (*la halle au blé*).

Directions <small>(See key for abbreviations)</small>

1 Leave Mortagne down the D938 and head R onto greenway past Restaurant de la Gare.

2 Coming into Le-Mêle-sur-Sarthe look out for a sign to the Base de Loisirs off the greenway if you want to pay a visit to the swimming lake.

Accommodation

To call a French number from the UK add 00 33 at the beginning and delete the first 0 of the French number.

1 CHAMBRE D'HÔTES LA MAISON PERVENCHE
61560 Böecé
02 33 28 07 00   gites-de-france-orne.com

2 LES CHAMBRES DE L'ORNE
La Fosse 61560 Böecé
02 33 83 64 13
les-chambres-de-lorne.e-monsite.com

3 LA MAISON DE PRINTEMPS
1 place de Tilleuls
61560 Bazoches-sur-Hoëne
02 50 77 11 49
lamaisondeprintemps.com
Sauna. One room only accommodating five people.

4 HÔTEL DE LA POSTE **
31 place du Général de Gaulle
61170 Le Mêle-sur-Sarthe
02 33 81 18 00
restauranthoteldelaposte.com

5 CAMPING CAMP INTERCOMMUNAL DE LA PRAIRIE
Lieu-dit La Bretèche 61770 Le Mêle-sur-Sarthe
02 33 27 18 74   cdcvalleedelahautesarthe.com
Open May – September. Apart from pitches they have a couple of chalets/pods.

Attractions

LE MÊLE-SUR-SARTHE LEISURE LAKE
Attractions include swimming and sailing in a lovely wooded setting.

Action sports addicts should check out the flyboarding and hoverboarding!

© Joël Damase

Typical greenway riding

i **Le Mêle-sur-Sarthe**
place Charles de Gaulle
02 33 27 63 97
le-mele-sur-sarthe.stationverte.com

Veloscenic

Alençon   © Joel Damase

3 Voie Verte ends here; R onto road and S/O next main road.

4 Head over the A28 motorway and first L onto minor road. Follow Voie Verte signs to eventually join greenway.

1 CHAMBRE D'HÔTES BOISAUBERT
61170 Marchemaisons
02 33 27 02 95   gites-de-boisaubert.com

2 AUBERGE NORMAND
rue du Pont de Londeau 61250 Valframbert
02 33 29 43 29   aubergenormande.wixsite.com

3 HOTEL F1 ALENÇON
Parc d'activités "Le Londeau", rue de Bel air,
61000 Cerisé
0891 70 51 58   accorhotels.com

4 HOTEL CAMPANILE ALENÇON
ZAT de Londeau 61250 Valframbert, Alençon
02 33 29 53 85   campanile.com

5 B&B HÔTEL ALENÇON NORD **
Pôle d'Activités d'Ecouves, Rue François Arago,
Valframbert, Alençon
08 92 78 80 02   hotel-bb.com

6 CHÂTEAU DE SARCEAUX
61250 Valframbert, Alençon
02 33 28 85 11 / 06 07 49 52 58
chateau-de-sarceaux.com
Luxury B&B in an eighteenth century château

△ 7 CAMPING D'ECOUVES ***
Ferme des Noyers
61250 Ecouves
02 33 28 75 02 06 08 70 14 63 ecouves.net

★ ARBORETUM DE ZONE HUMIDE
Collection of wetland trees. Further to the west is a swimming pool and other attractions on the outskirts of Alençon include a skating rink and concert hall.

Veloscenic

Alençon

RUE DE L'ADORATION
RUE D'ISIGNY AUVERGER
RUE DU LANCEMENT
BOULEVARD DE STRASBOURG
D 112
RUE DU TEMPS DU HUSSARD
AVENUE DE BASINGSTOKE
D 438
AVENUE DE QUAKENBR

5

RUE DES GENETTES
RUE DE L'ÉCUSSON
RUE JULLIEN
Parc Cerisey-Germond
Monastère des Clarisses d'Alençon
RUE DE LA DEMI-LUNE
Parc de la Préfecture
RUE DE LA PYRAMIDE
MBK
Cycles Josse
AVENUE WILSON
1 **2** **3**

RUE D'BETTELLES
Bibliothèque Municipale
Lacemaking Museum
RUE DE L'ISLE
RUE LANGLOIS
RUE DES GRANDES POTERIES
COURS CLEMENCEAU
RUE DU PUITS
RUE DES MARCHERIES
RUE SAINT-BLAISE
Martin Family House
RUE ODOLANT DESNOS
RUE DEMÈES
6 **4**
D 438

5

RUE DE BRETAGNE
7
6
RUE DES FILLES NOTRE-DAME
RUE DU CYGNE
Corn Exchange
RUE AUX SIEURS
Alençon
GRANDE RUE
RUE CAZAULT
RUE DES CAPUCINS
PLACE DU GÉNÉRAL BONNET
Temple
RUE CAZAULT

7
RUE DU VAL NOBLE
RUE DU MARÉCHAL DE LATTRE DE
RUE DU BERCAIL
Basilique Notre-Dame
RUE BOURDON
RUE PIQUET
BOULEVARD DE LA RÉPUBLIQUE

Château des Ducs
Carmel d'Alençon
GRANDE RUE
Jacques Goupil Art Gallery
Parc de la Providence
Balade au Fil de l'Eau
QUAI HENRI DUNANT
La Sarthe

Église St-Léonard
RUE DE LA FUIE DES VIGNES

8
La Sarthe
BOULEVARD
RUE DES FOSSÉS DE L'ÉCHELLE
RUE DE LA SENAUTÉRIE
RUE DE L'ISLE
RUE ARISTIDE BRIAND
RUE SÉGRIN
D 438
RUE DE L'ISLE

Montsort
RUE SAINT-PIERRE
RUE DU CLANGE
RUE DU MANS
PLACE DU CHAMP DE
RUE DU CHAMP
Église St-Pierre de Montsort
Bayi Cycles
BOULEVARD DE LA RÉPUBLIQUE
RUE DE L'ÉCOLE NORMALE

RUE DES BASSES-RUELLES
RUE DE GESNES
RUE SULPICE
Chapelle Notre-Dame-Lorette

N

0 Metres 100 200 300
0 Yards 100 200 300

RUE DE LA RILLE
D 955
AVENUE DE KOUTIALA
D 438
D 955
AVENUE RHIN
AVENUE SAINT-DENIS
La Sarthe

ℹ️ **Alençon**
Maison d'Ozé
02 33 80 66 33   02 33 80 66 32
visitalencon.com

5 Greenway ends at av de Quakenbruck. R here and immediate R over railway bridge onto cycle path. L at main road.
6 2nd R at next R/B onto rue Saint-Blaise. This brings you to the central square and the impressive church of Notre-Dame.

To leave Alençon carry on past the church onto Grand Rue then 4th R onto rue du Val Noble.
7 R onto rue des Filles Sainte-Claire and S/O in car park area by Corn Exchange then L to R/B and second R here onto rue de Bretagne.

1 HÔTEL LE NORMANDIE *
16 rue Denis Papin 61000 Alençon
02 33 29 00 51 hoteldenormandiealencon.fr

2 HÔTEL DE PARIS *
26 rue Denis Papin 61000 Alençon
02 33 29 01 64 hoteldeparis-alencon.com

3 HÔTEL DES DUCS ***
50 avenue Wilson 61000 Alençon
02 33 29 03 93 hoteldesducs-alencon.fr

4 HÔTEL LE HUSSARD
22 place du Général Charles de Gaulle
61000 Alençon
02 33 27 19 30 lehussard-alencon.com

5 HÔTEL IBIS ALENÇON ***
13 Place Auguste Poulet Malassis 61000 Alençon
02 33 80 67 67 accorhotels.com

6 CHAMBRES D'HOTES LA HULOTTE
47 rue Albert 1er 61000 Alençon
02 33 32 28 11 gites-de-france.com

7 HOTEL LE CHAPEAU ROUGE***
3 boulevard Duchamp 61000 Alençon
02 33 29 49 37 lechapeaurouge.net

8 CAMPING MUNICIPAL DE GUÉRAMÉ
65 rue de Guerame 61000 Alençon
02 33 26 21 02

LACEMAKING MUSEUM
History of the local industry and a workshop showing how it was once made - in incredible detail and by hand.

MARTIN FAMILY HOUSE
Birthplace of Saint Thérèse of Lisieux, one of France's most revered saints.

L'ÉGLISE NOTRE DAME
An impressive building in its own right whose stained glass is probably its finest point.

CHÂTEAU DES DUCS
Only a couple of towers remain of the original medieval structure. The building was a prison until 2010. Though private at the time of writing, it is still an impressive facade and there are plans for the city to acquire the building and open it up to the public.

HALLE AU BLÉ
Imposing corn exchange.

JACQUES GOUPIL ART GALLERY
Exhibitions of modern and regional art.

BALADE AU FIL DE L'EAU
Boat trips along the lovely Sarthe river.

SNCF Alençon is on the south-north rail line between Le Mans and Caen. Returning to Paris involves taking a local train to Le Mans then booking your bike on the TGV. The whole trip should take between 1 hour 40mins and 2 hours. To access the nearest station to the end of the route, Pontorson, takes between 4 and 5 hours and means changes at Caen or Lison (local trains only) or Le Mans and Rennes (TGV to Rennes meaning you must book your bike on the service in advance).

Veloscenic

Bagnoles

Alençon ~ Bagnoles-de-l'Orne

Undulating roads take you through beautiful landscapes of the Normandy-Maine Regional Natural Park and the forest of Écouves; there are some stiff climbs here and remote feeling, dense forest. Carrouges Castle is an impressive granite, brick and slate construction which also hosts the Natural Park Centre and its terrace is perfect for a picnic, the approach to its highly stylised facade one of the most memorable sections on the whole Veloscenic route.

Then there is the famous thermal spa of Bagnoles-de-l'Orne. A haven for relaxation in the heart of the Andaines forest, this spa resort boasts wonderful Belle Époque architecture and thermal baths and a glorious town centre lake.

Route Info

Distance 53 kilometres / 33 miles

Terrain & Route Surface Wonderfully quiet roads with an extended climb up the Sarthon valley to Carrouges. A traffic-free alternative nearly all the way from Alençon to Bagnoles is planned for the future.

Off-road 1%

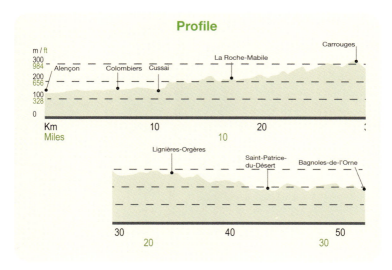

Profile

Don't Miss

• A small, low-key but very attractive stop off is the hamlet of **La Roche-Mabile**, complete with church and an attractive centre.

• **Carrouges** is best known for its distinctive château, dating partly from the 14th century. It combines an austere fortress with a comfortable residence.

The original defences were destroyed by English forces during the Hundred Years War but rebuilt afterwards by Jean Blosset, grand seneschal of Normandy, in the 15th century.

In the 16th century, the family of Le Veneur de Tillières owned Carrouges and extended it several times with the addition of a gatehouse, the western bastion, and the grand apartments. The interior was remodelled in the 18th century, when the music room was built. The last Le Veneur sold the château to the French state, and from 1944 it was restored. It is now managed by the *Centre des monuments nationaux* and is open to the public. There are also 25 acres of gardens.

Also here is **La Ferme Ornée de Carrouges -** over seven hectares of bocage gardened in the style of farm tableaus with seven themed gardens.

Veloscenic at Carrouges

Bagnoles-de-l'Orne

The Normandy-Maine Natural Park centre is also at Carrouges, combining visitor centre, museum, tourist information, local produce shop and exhibitions of ancient craftsmanship. There's a picnic area on site too.

• **Bagnoles-de-l'Orne** breaks with the rural and often very historic character of much of its Norman surroundings.

Its main business is to provide thermal bath treatments and relaxing holidays to wealthy visitors as it has been doing since around the turn of the 19th century from when many of the buildings here date. Most of the relaxing takes place around the lovely central lake which, in the manner of many Belle Époque areas of France, also features a casino. Also worth a look are the massive park and arboretum surrounding the lovely town hall (château de la Roche Bagnoles), the church of Sacré-Cœur and the Roc au Chien, near the eponymous hotel.

Veloscenic

Directions (See key for abbreviations)

1 See pages 90-91 for directions out of Alençon centre to rue de Bretagne. S/O a R/B 1st R onto rue Giroye, bending 90 degrees L to T junction. R here onto pavement cycle lane.
2 After 0.7km on cycle lane (including crossing major junction) L onto Sente du Milieu. Split R onto path into open countryside.
3 R when path meets road at Damigny centre (note future traffic-free option will carry straight on here in future - planned for 2019).
4 L a R/B in Colombiers to briefly join D1 then R back onto D204 just over small bridge.
5 L onto D532 S Cussai. S/O D2 in Cussai staying on D532.
6 R onto D250 S La Roche-Mabile. Follow D250 through La Roche -Mabile.
7 L onto D226 S Saint-Ellier-les-Bois.
8 Split R and drop and climb steeply to T-junction and R, rejoining D250 all the way to Carrouges.
9 S/O R/B joining D909 on edge of Carrouges. L onto the long drop towards the Château itself (town centre on your R before the turn). Pass Château to your L, joining D16 leaving Carrouges.

Accommodation

To call a French number from the UK add 00 33 at the beginning and delete the first 0 of the French number.

1 CHAMBRE D'HÔTE LE CROCQ
61250 Colombiers 02 33 26 70 91
https://manoirlecrocq.jimdo.com

2 MAISON D'HÔTES LA BRUYÈRE
La Chapelle 61420 Gandelain
06 21 03 55 8

3 CHAMBRES D'HÔTE LE CHEVAL BLANC
14 rue du Docteur Tremblin 61320 Carrouges
06 84 67 17 87 entremeretcampagne.fr

4 HOTEL LE RELAIS DE CARROUGES
10 rue Sainte-Marguerite 61320 Carrouges
02 33 32 15 80

5 LA FERME DE CORINNE ET HUGUES
DESFRIÈCHES (4km / 2.5 miles n of Carrouges)
L'Aunay 61320 Ste Marguerite de Carrouges
02 33 26 39 86
www.calvados-huguesdesfrieches.com

Attractions

⭐ CARROUGES
See Don't Miss. E-bike hire is available at the information centre of the château.

⭐ LA FERME ORNÉE DE CARROUGES
See Don't Miss.

⭐ BELVÉDÈRE DU MONT DES AVALOIRS
18 metre tall viewing tower at the highest point in western France with great tree top panoramas.

⭐ LA FERME DE CORINNE ET HUGUES
DESFRIÈCHES Working cider farm. See **5**

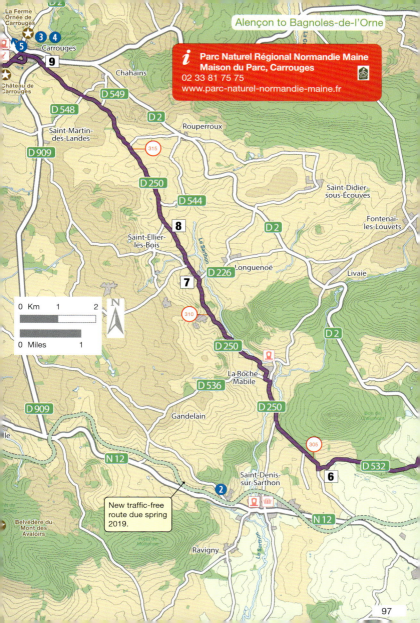

Parc Naturel Régional Normandie Maine
Maison du Parc, Carrouges
02 33 81 75 75
www.parc-naturel-normandie-maine.fr

La Ferme Ornée de Carrouges

Carrouges

Château de Carrouges

Chahains

D 549

D 548

D 2

Saint-Martin-des-Landes

D 909

Rouperroux

315

D 250

D 544

Saint-Didier-sous-Écouves

Fontenai-les-Louvets

D 2

Saint-Ellier-les-Bois

Le Sarthon

D 226

Longuenoë

Livaie

310

D 2

D 250

La Roche-Mabile

D 536

Gandelain

D 250

305

D 532

D 909

N 12

New traffic-free route due spring 2019.

Saint-Denis-sur-Sarthon

Le Sarthon

N 12

Belvédère du Mont des Avaloirs

Ravigny

0 Km 1 2

N

0 Miles 1

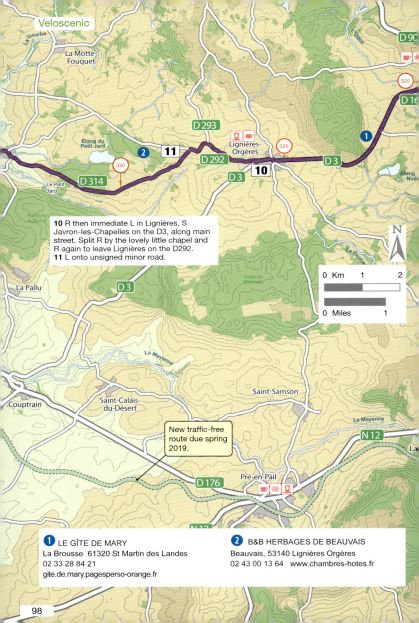

10 R then immediate L in Lignières, S Javron-les-Chapelles on the D3, along main street. Split R by the lovely little chapel and R again to leave Lignières on the D292.
11 L onto unsigned minor road.

New traffic-free route due spring 2019.

1 LE GÎTE DE MARY
La Brousse 61320 St Martin des Landes
02 33 28 84 21
gite.de.mary.pagesperso-orange.fr

2 B&B HERBAGES DE BEAUVAIS
Beauvais, 53140 Lignières Orgères
02 43 00 13 64   www.chambres-hotes.fr

Briouze Spur

Saint-André-

D 21

D 924

Briouze

Le Val du Breuil

Guillame Boulay

Marais du
Grand Hazé

Saint-Hilaire-
de-Briouze

Pointel

Le Ménil-
de-Briouze

D 21

D 20

D 19

i **Pays du Briouze**
Espace Culturel du Houlme
place du Général de Gaulle
02 33 62 81 50

Lignou

Faverolles

0 Km 1 2

0 Miles 1

N

★ MARAIS DU GRAND HAZÉ
200 hectares of wetland and
pasture with Camargue horses
and Highland cattle.

Lonlay-le-
Tesson

Le Grais

Etang
de la Lande
Forêt

SNCF Direct but infrequent
trains from Briouze to
Paris Montparnasse taking 2 and
a half to 3 hours. You can also get
to Pontorson at the western end of
the route but trains are again very
infrequent.

D 19

du-Désert

D 916

Beauvain

D 18

La
Ferté-Macé

D 402

La Ferté-Macé

Tendance Vélo
& AGM

D 53

See overleaf for details of
spur link from Bagnoles-
de-l'orne

D 916

La
Ferté-Macé

nt-Michel-
s-Andaines

D 908

D 908

D 402

✪ BAGNOLES-DE-L'ORNE

See Don't Miss. There is also the Arboretum Parc du Château surrounding the town hall. The Casino has a restaurant, bar, cinema, cabaret etc. A vélorail (pedal operated railcarts on former rail line) runs five km through the forest to La Ferté Macé. As a spa town there are many health spas too. At Le Bois there are tree walks, zip wires and the like for adrenaline addicts. If you fancy more outdoor activity there is an open air swimming pool, an archery range and a selection of indoor and outdoor tennis courts.

✪ CHÂTEAU DE COUTERNE

16th / 17th century château with grounds. A costume exhibition is open in the summer.

✪ AÉROCLUB D'ANDAINES

Pleasure flights in the club's aircraft.

✪ BAGNOLES DE POM

Cider farm with shop and open day visits from time to time.

---

12 Follow the D314 all the way to St-Patrice and split L by the church, passing the excellent picnic shelter and toilets.
13 At X-rds S/O signed Chappelle St-Antoine.
14 Climb into the Andaines forest on route Forestière de Cossé.
15 S/O D270.
16 At the D20 the road to the R takes you to La Ferté-Macé. The main route is S/O.

17 S/O D916 and branch L and L again at the Carrefour de l'Épinette to come onto excellent roadside cycle lanes.
18 Coming into Bagnoles follow the Suivre Golf signs. Cycle tracks bring you to R/B at avenue de La Ferté-Macé by the tourist office. Bear R and S/O R/B with fountain onto rue des Casinos and pass the lake on the R. R at R/B S Domfront to climb out of town on D235.

---

❶ AUBERGE D'ANDAINES *
route de Bagnoles-de-l'Orne
61600 la Ferté-Macé.
02 33 37 20 28   aubergeandaines.com
Bikes kept in hotel on ground floor

❷ HÔTEL LE NORMANDIE *
2 avenue Paul Lemuet 61140 Bagnoles-de-l'Orne
02 33 30 71 30   hotel-le-normandie.com

❸ O GAYOT
2 avenue de La Ferté-Macé
61140 Bagnoles-de-l'Orne
02 33 38 44 01   02 33 38 47 71   ogayot.fr

❹ BOIS JOLI *
12 avenue Philippe du Rozier
61140 Bagnoles-de-l'Orne
02 33 37 92 77   hotelboisjoli.com

❺ B'O COTTAGE RÉSIDENCE
Boulevard de la Gatinière
61140 Bagnoles-de-l'Orne
0 811 90 22 33   bo-cottage.com

❻ LES CAMÉLIAS *
6 avenue du Château de Couterne
61140 Bagnoles-de-l'Orne
02 33 37 93 11 / 02 33 37 48 32
cameliashotel.com

❼ HÔTEL DE LA POTINIERE
2 rue des Casinos 61140 Bagnoles-de-l'Orne
02 33 30 65 00   hoteldelapotiniere.com

❽ HÔTEL LE ROC AU CHIEN *
10-12 rue du Professeur Louvel
61140 Bagnoles-de-l'Orne
02 33 37 97 33   hotelrocauchien.fr

❾ HÔTEL DE TESSÉ
1 avenue de la Baillée
61140 Bagnoles-de-l'Orne
02 33 30 80 07   hoteldetesse.com

❿ HÔTEL SPA DU BERYL *
1 rue des Casinos
61140 Bagnoles-de-l'Orne
02 33 38 44 44
hotel-bagnoles.com

⓫ B'O RÉSIDENCE DES THERMES
rue du Professeur Louvel
61140 Bagnoles-de-l'Orne
0 811 90 22 33
bo-cottage.com/fr/bo-residence.html

⓬ CAMPING MUNICIPAL DE LA VÉE *
5, avenue du Président Coty
61140 Bagnoles-de-l'Orne
02 33 37 87 45   campingbagnolesdelorne.com

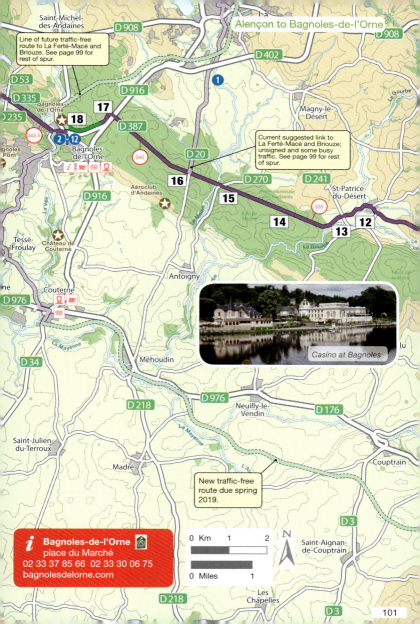

Saint-Michel-des-Andaines

D 908

D 908

Line of future traffic-free route to La Ferté-Macé and Briouze. See page 99 for rest of spur.

D 402

D 53

D 916

1

Magny-le-Désert

D 335

D 235

Bagnoles-de-l'Orne

17

18

D 387

343.5

2 **12**

Bagnoles-de-l'Orne

340

D 20

Current suggested link to La Ferté-Macé and Briouze; unsigned and some busy traffic. See page 99 for rest of spur.

16

D 270

D 241

St-Patrice-du-Désert

Aéroclub d'Andaines

15

335

14

13 **12**

D 916

Tessé-Froulay

Château de Couterne

La Vée

Antoigny

La Gourbe

Couterne

D 976

Méhoudin

Casino at Bagnoles

D 34

La Mayenne

D 218

D 976

Neuilly-le-Vendin

D 176

Saint-Julien-du-Terroux

Madré

New traffic-free route due spring 2019.

Couptrain

D 3

i **Bagnoles-de-l'Orne**
place du Marché
02 33 37 85 66   02 33 30 06 75
bagnolesdelorne.com

0 Km   1   2

N

Saint-Aignan-de-Couptrain

0 Miles   1

Les Chapelles

D 218

D 3

Leaving Domfront

Bagnoles-de-l'Orne ~ Saint-Hilaire

On leaving Bagnoles-de-l'Orne, the route wends its way along small roads on the edge of the Andaines forest before entering the charming medieval town of Domfront, which has a lovely old centre. Mortain is a 2.5 mile trip off the greenway and gives you the chance to visit the impressive waterfalls and Mortain's old centre.

Finally, Saint-Hilaire-du-Harcouët is a really attractive small town with a good range of facilities and activities.

Route Info

Distance 60 kilometres / 37 miles

Terrain & Route Surface A long road climb on a fast D road precedes a great forest section on a tarmac, virtually traffic-free access road before urban roads bring you into Domfront. From here an excellent quality crushed stone surface trail takes you all the way to Saint-Hilaire-du-Harcouët and beyond.

Off-road 64%

Profile

Don't Miss

• **Domfront** has a wonderful medieval centre, full of half-timbered houses and featuring a lovely central square. The old centre is linked by a footbridge to the remains of what must once have been an impregnable castle, partly the effort of Henry I. There are great panoramic views from the castle ruins today over the hilly, wooded countryside hereabouts - quite a contrast to previous landscapes. At the other end of town lies the neo-Byzantine (actually1920s but curiously ancient looking from a distance at least) church of St-Julien, with Art Noveau interior. In the valley below lies the ancient church of Notre-Dame sur l'Eau where Thomas à Becket came to say mass in 1166. The Eau in question is the lovely Varenne river which runs through an attractive little valley to the west of the castle and is used briefly by Veloscenic before it finds the traffic-free trail once again on its way to Saint-Hilaire.

It also has a slight international tourist flavour about it.

Domfront's medieval centre

Saint-Hilaire-du-Harcouët

• At Barenton you will find the **Musée du Poiré**, housed in a typical Normandy farm with its clay walls and timber frame. It celebrates the work of the cider maker and is surrounded by apple and pear orchards.

• The detour off the greenway to Mortain gives you the chance to visit the largest waterfall in northwest France, the **Grande Cascade**. It falls more than 20m, and there are smaller falls, part of the tumultuous course of the river Cance in the area.

• The centre of **Saint-Hilaire-du-Harcouët** is dominated by the church, bombed to a roofless condition in WWII, but restored. Much of the rest of the town was literally blown to smithereens during the liberation of 1944 (estimates are that around 78% of it was totally destroyed) but restored to its wonderful present condition. Near the church stands an old 12th century tower, once part of larger Norman fortifications. It now houses unusual modern murals though it is rarely open. It overlooks an attractive lake and parkland.

Directions (See key for abbreviations)

1 Split R off D235 onto D335, S Domfront.
2 Before meeting main road head L across car park area onto route Forestière de Lucé.
3 At split at Carrefour de la Roche keep L.
4 Route Forestière ends at T-junction. L here and immediate R S Perrou.
5 Past church in Perrou R onto C2 S Domfront.
6 Entering Domfront first R up chemin de la Cosnière.
7 R at T-junction and climb steeply to main road (D908) and L.

8 Split R up D103 and follow towards church spire in town centre.
9 Pass church and S/O down Domfront main street to castle. Bend L there and descend: EASY TO MISS - head across road onto steps with cycle ramp alongside (rue du Château) then R onto rue Notre-Dame.
10 EASY TO MISS R off rue Notre-Dame onto single track path, descending across road and over river. Meet greenway and L (Velo Francette cycle route is R which you don't want).

Attractions

⭐ ARBORETUM DE L'ÉTOILE D'ANDAINES
Two km walking loop through 66 types of tree.

⭐ TOUR DE BONVOULOIR
Spectacular chapel, tower and dovecote in the Fôret de Lancelot du Lac.

⭐ DOMFRONT
See Don't Miss. The Comte Louis de Lauriston cellars offer the tasting and sale of Calvados

cider, poiré and pommeau. The Musée Charles Léandre is a local history museum in the town hall. Tertre Sainte-Anne are cliffs and hills used for climbing, walking, mountain biking and a host of other outdoor activities.

⭐ BAGNOLES DE POM
Working cider farm with sales of their produce.

⭐ MANOIR DE LA GUYARDIÈRE
Picturesque 17th century house with grounds and lakeside walk.

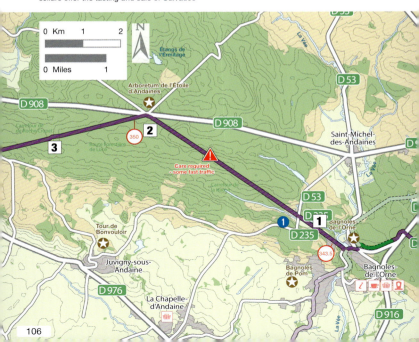

Velofrancette route heads north from Domfront to Flers (see overleaf).

Bagnoles-de-l'Orne to Saint-Hilaire

Domfront
12, place de la Roirie
02 33 38 53 97 / 02 33 37 40 27
ot-domfront.com

Accommodation

To call a French number from the UK add 00 33 at the beginning and delete the first 0 of the French number.

1 LE MANOIR DU LYS
route du Juvigny 61140 Bagnoles de l'Orne
02 33 37 80 69 manoir-du-lys.com

2 HÔTEL DE LA CROIX DES LANDES
route de la Ferté Macé 61700 Domfront

3 CHAMBRES D'HÔTES BELLE VALLÉE
Belle Vallée Domfront 61700
02 33 37 05 71 belle-vallee.net

4 NUMERO CINQ
5 rue Montgomery 61700 Domfront
02 33 30 19 36 facebook.com/numerocinq.domfront

5 HÔTEL DE FRANCE**
7 rue du Mont Saint Michel 61700 Domfront
02 33 38 51 44 hoteldefrance-fr.com

6 LE RELAIS ST MICHEL
5 rue du Mont Saint-Michel 61700 Domfront
01 45 84 83 84

7 CHAMBRE D'HOTES BELLE VUE
10 rue de la Gare 61700 Domfront
09 53 06 04 85 / 06 19 11 54 99

8 CAMPING À LA FERME SOUS LES POIRIERS
La Touche 61700 Domfront
02 33 37 03 99 / 06 63 07 55 50
yourte-souslespoiriers.com
Organic farm produce available

9 CAMPING MUNICIPAL DU CHAMP PASSAIS **
rue du Champ Passais 61700 Domfront
02 33 37 37 66 camping-municipal-domfront.jimdo.com

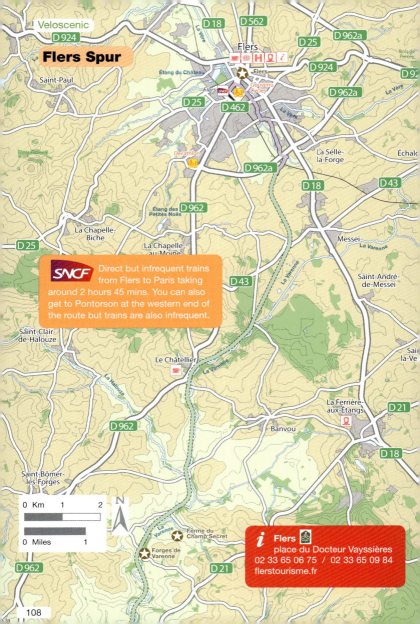

Veloscenic

D 924

Flers Spur

Saint-Paul

Flers

Étang du Château

Flers

D 25

D 462

D 18

D 562

D 25

D 962a

D 924

D 962a

La Selle-la-Forge

Échalo

La Vere

Decathlon

D 962a

D 18

D 43

Étang des Petites Noës

D 962

La Chapelle-Biche

D 25

La Chapelle-au-Moine

Messei

La Varenne

Saint-André-de-Messei

La Varenne

SNCF Direct but infrequent trains from Flers to Paris taking around 2 hours 45 mins. You can also get to Pontorson at the western end of the route but trains are also infrequent.

D 43

Saint-Clair-de-Halouze

Le Châtellier

La Varenne

La Halouze

Sai la-Ve

D 962

La Ferrière-aux-Étangs

D 21

Banvou

D 18

Saint-Bômer-les-Forges

0 Km 1 2

N

0 Miles 1

La Varenne

Ferme du Champ-Secret

Forges de Varenne

D 962

D 21

Flers
place du Docteur Vayssières
02 33 65 06 75 / 02 33 65 09 84
flerstourisme.fr

⭐ **PARC DES FORGES DE VARENNE**
16th century iron forge and park

⭐ **FERME DU CHAMP SECRET**
Cheese and dairy farm

⭐ **FLERS**
The château museum (built in the 18th century to aid the Chouans - those still loyal to the monarchy after the French Revolution had abolished it) has fine arts and history on display and the Église St-Jean is an attractive mid-nineteenth century church. La Chapelle du Souvenir is an amazing Art Deco church built in 1926 to commemorate the war dead. There is also a modern mosque built by the Franco-Turkish community.

Serge ULM Flers de l'Orne offers introductory microlight and small aircraft flights.

Domfront

 CAMPING LA BONELIÈRE
La Bonelière 61350 Saint-Mars-d'Egrennie
06 03 57 46 73
gitecampinglaboneliere.com

 GÎTE LA DIFFERENCE - LE PRESSOIR
61700 DOMFRONT
02 33 65 03 23   www.difference-pressoir.com
Sauna and swimming pool available

 CHAMBRES D'HÔTES
10 rue du Prieuré 50720 Saint-Cyr-du-Bailleul
02 33 59 43 89 / 06 65 32 33 33
antoinette.hardy@hotmail.fr

 GÎTES DE FRANCE LA GARE
La Gare 50720 Saint-Cyr-du-Bailleul
06 60 13 72 15
gites.mortainais@msm-normandie.fr

 CHAMBRES D'HÔTES
115 rue de la Libération 50720 Barenton
02 33 51 57 44 / 06 30 16 27 01
(on map opposite bottom)

 MAISON VOIE VERTE
50140 Bion
02 33 50 07 27   maisonvoieverte.com

GRAND CASCADE, MORTAIN SPUR
See Don't Miss

LA PETITE CHAPELLE SANT-MICHEL
Dramatic hilltop setting with stunning views.
Scene of fierce WWII fighting.

BLANCHE ABBEY, MORTAIN SPUR
A 12th century abbey, now disused but still a
magnificent piece of architecture.

MANOIR DE LA BONELIÈRE
16th century house and gardens (Sundays only)

CAVE NORMANDE
Farm and shop selling Calvados, cider and
pommeau.

MUSÉE DU POIRÉ
Museum and shop to the local pear based drink

11 R at split in trail (L is Vélo Francette cycle
route south).
12 Near the Sélune river there is a link
to Barenton (small working town with a
supermarket in the centre) via the Musée du
Poiré and a minor road link back to the trail.
13 Tour de Manche and Petit Tour de Manche
cycle routes head R, off main Veloscenic route,
up a greenway to Vire, Mortain and Romagny).

Directions to Mortain
13m Having headed R up the signed greenway
head across D977 and continue up greenway.
14m At X-roads ('cascades' waterfalls straight
on and Mortain centre to R).

1 HÔTEL-RESTAURANT LES CLOSEAUX PHIL
50140 Romagny
02 33 61 41 45   lescloseauxphil.com

2 HÔTEL DE LA POSTE
1 Place des Arcades, 50140 Mortain
02 33 59 00 05   hoteldelaposte-mortain.fr

3 GÎTES DE FRANCE LE PARC
Le Parc, Bion 50140 Mortain-Bocage
02 99 88 34 78 / 06 10 91 42 35
leparc-clairet.com

4 CAMPING MUNICIPAL LES CASCADES
Place du Château 50140 Mortain-Bocage
02 33 79 30 30   ville-mortain.fr

Mortain
rue du Bourglopin
02 33 59 19 74   mortainais-tourisme.org

Veloscenic

14 Saint-Hilaire centre is L up the D977 which the greenway crosses.

1 HÔTEL DE L'AGRICULTURE
79 – 81 rue Waldeck Rousseau
50600 Saint Hilaire-du-Harcouët
02 33 49 10 60   hoteldelagriculture.com

2 HÔTEL LE CYGNE
99 rue Waldeck Rousseau
50600 Saint Hilaire-du-Harcouët
02 33 49 11 84   brit-hotel.fr

3 HÔTEL LE LION D'OR
120 rue de la République
50600 Saint-Hilaire-du-Harcouët
02 33 89 55 83   www.hotelleliondor.com

4 CAMPING MUNICIPAL LA SÉLUNE **
rue de Marly 50600 Saint-Hilaire-du-Harcouët
02 33 49 43 74   st-hilaire.fr

✪ ST-HILAIRE-DU-HARCOUËT

See Don't Miss. The Plan d'Eau du Prieuré is a delightful and large lake area with various activities.

Compact town centre with all facilities including cinema and swimming pool.

Trail riding near Milly

© Joel Damase

Mont-Saint-Michel seen from Veloscenic
as it passes through the bay's hinterland.

Saint-Hilaire ~ Mont-Saint-Michel

On the last stage of Veloscenic, the greenway snakes its way to the mouth of the Sélune river, passing highly attractive Ducey, with its imposing Château de Montgommery. Pontaubault marks the start of small minor roads which offer a myriad of viewpoints across the bay towards the silhouette of Mont-Saint-Michel , the end of the route. The "Marvel of the West" and its bay, the theatre for the the biggest tides in Europe, have been listed by UNESCO as a World Heritage Site since 1979. A visit to the island abbey and village will end your journey in breathtaking style.

Route Info

Distance 51 kilometres / 31.5 miles

Terrain & Route Surface More high quality crushed stone greenway ends at Pontaubault and a flat section of minor roads leads to several climbs through small villages before a descent to the tarmac greenway down to Mont-Saint-Michel.

Off-road 47%

Profile

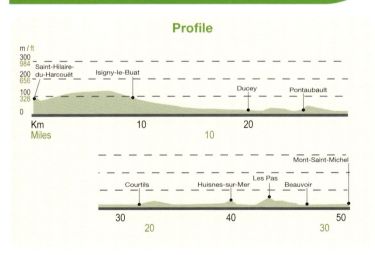

Don't Miss

• **Ducey** is a small yet charming town most notable for its 17th century **Château des Montgommery**. Its building was started by Gabriel II of Montgommery who actually took over Mont-Saint-Michel for a very short period during the religious wars of the 17th century. By the 1980s the Château des Montgommery was in decay and surrounded by a disused factory, but was subsequently lovingly restored after the town purchased it.

• **Mont-Saint-Michel** is known as the Marvel of the West in France and once you have set eyes on it you will see why.

Rising like a vision out of the bay, the abbey sits atop the buildings around its base that house the 50 or so people who still live here. Its history dates back to the eighth century but the most impressive buildings were grafted on afterwards. In 966 Richard I gave the abbey to the Benedictines after which it became a centre of learning and later something of a medieval fortress. During the Hundred Years War in the 15th century it withstood several sieges from the English. Today there is one access, the Porte de l'Avancée which leads to the one main street, the Grande Rue, lined with shops aimed fairly and squarely at tourists as you might expect (nearby Pontorson is a more relaxed and affordable place to stay and eat than anywhere in the immediate vicinity of the abbey itself).

The Abbey buildings themselves are known as 'la Merveille' or the marvel, not surprising for a collection of buildings that were described by Maupassant as being 'as vast as a town'. There is a church and a monastery.

Château des Montgommery

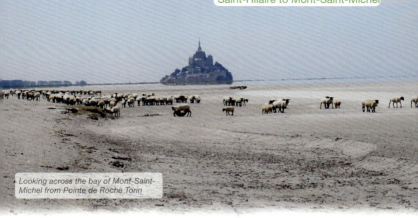

Looking across the bay of Mont-Saint-Michel from Pointe de Roche Torin

• **The bay of Mont-Saint-Michel** is just as spectacular as the abbey with its 15 metre tidal range covering and hiding a vast expanse of sands. When the tide is out you can walk around the abbey though straying too far can be dangerous. A new causeway with cycle lanes and shuttle access was built in 2014 which has helped in reducing silting up around the causeway itself; it was feared at one point that the sands around the island would completely silt up and that it would be an island no longer; it was projected that by 2040 the Mont would simply be surrounded by a grassy bank.

The causeway was itself part of a larger project costing around £144 million that saw the masses of car parking at the base of the rock banished and the old problematically 'solid' causeway dismantled. Now shuttle buses transport visitors the mile or so from the nearest car parks. Cyclists are restricted from cycling on the causeway to the Mont at certain times of the day, and when bike access is not allowed they are advised to leave their bikes at bike parks also around a mile away from the Mont (note luggage and bike storage facilities closed at time of writing for security reasons). For more info on access and services see the following which includes a good site plan showing parking and transport arrangements: **bienvenueaumontsaintmichel.com** The dam you see here today and can walk over was also part of the project and is used to build up a head of water before releasing it to flush away any silt that is starting to build up around the Mont.

The **Mascaret** is a tidal bore up the rivers flowing into the bay caused by the high tides around the Mont. If you want to experience more distant but equally impressive vistas of the Mont in all its glory amidst the bay, Veloscenic passes by **Pointe de Roche Torin** around 4 miles after leaving Pontaubault. There are also more elevated vistas from nearby Huisnes-sur-Mer and its German war cemetery.

117

Accommodation

To call a French number from the UK add 00 33 at the beginning and delete the first 0 of the French number.

1 LA MOTTE
8 – 10, route Nationale 50600 Virey
02 33 51 00 84   lamottebandb.fr

2 CHAMBRES D'HÔTES LA JAUNAIS
15 route Bliais 50600 Virey
02 33 49 14 75 / 06 62 61 17 21
jyermeneux@wanadoo.fr

3 GITES D'ÉTAPE
4 rue du Pain d'Avaine 50540 Isigny-le-Buat
06 84 74 25 27

4 CHAMBRES D'HÔTES LA CHEVALLERIE
Chalandrey Ducey 50540 Isigny-le-Buat
02 33 60 40 97

Attractions

✪ LE JARDIN DU CASSEL
Provides flowers for the florists at Isigny-le-Buat and the market at Granville .
Open to the public to look around in season.

✪ CHAPELLE NOTRE-DAME DE LA MISÉRICORDE ET DU ROSAIRE
Isigny-le-Buat

Traffic-free trail west of St-Hilaire

Directions (See key for abbreviations)

1 Ducey S off trail L up D78.
2 The trail ends as you see the disused rail bridge ahead. Descend to road and L into Pontaubault. R at next junction (town centre to L). Next L before river onto D113.

3 R onto D313 then shortly R again onto D313ᴱ S La Grève and La Roche Torin.

---

1 THE BLUE HOUSE B & B
25 Le Pavement 50220 Ducey   02 33 70 76 90

2 BEST WESTERN LE MOULIN DE DUCEY ***
1 grande rue 50220 Ducey-Les Cheris
02 33 60 25 25   moulindeducey.com

3 AUBERGE DE LA SÉLUNE **
2 rue St Germain 50220 Ducey
02 33 48 90 30   selune.com

4 CHAMBRES D'HÔTES LES SOURCES
5 Lentille 50220 Poilley
02 33 68 21 89   chambresdhoteslessourcesmanche.fr

ACCOMMODATION NOTE AVRANCHES SPUR:
Lots of accommodation at St-Quentin-sur-le-Homme, Le Val-Saint-Père and Avranches north of the route, including:

8 GÎTE DE LA MARRONNIÈRE
7b Argennes 50300 Le Val-Saint-Père
02 33 68 27 48   gitelamarronniere.free.fr

5 CHAMBRES D'HÔTES LE BOIS DE CRÉPI
2 Le Bois de Crépi 50220 Poilley
02 33 48 34 68 / 06 65 31 99 99

▲ **6** CAMPING LA VALLÉE DE LA SÉLUNE
7 rue Maréchal Leclerc 50220 Pontaubault
02 33 60 39 00   campselune.com/index2.htm

7 CHAMBRES D'HÔTES LE MÉE PROVOST
Le Mée Provost 50220 Céaux
02 33 60 49 03   normandie-tourisme.fr

9 HÔTEL LES TREIZE ASSIETTES ***
route de la Quintine 50300 Val Saint Père
02 33 89 03 03   hotel-le-saint-michel.com

10 MAISON D'HÔTES LES VALLÉES
12 route des Vallées
50220 Saint-Quentin-sur-le-Homme
02 33 60 61 51   lesvallees.com

✪ DUCEY
See Don't Miss. Lovely little compact centre with plenty of eating opportunities. To the south of Ducey lies Les Bois d'Ardennes, an ancient forest full of interesting wildlife, including Atlantic salmon in the river Sélune.

✪ AVRANCHES
Sizeable town with museums of art and history and one containing the manuscripts from Mont-Saint-Michel (The Scriptorial). Also firms offering guided walks around the bay. Some attractive gardens too.

Meet the river at Pontaubault   © Joel Damase

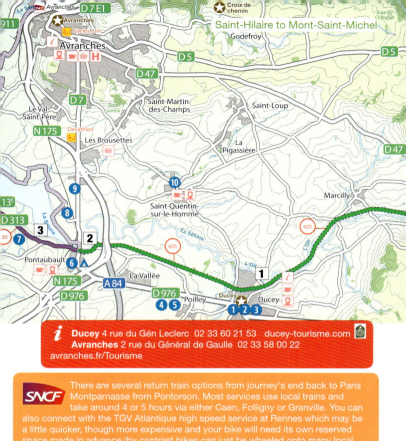

Saint-Hilaire to Mont-Saint-Michel

---

i **Ducey** 4 rue du Gén Leclerc 02 33 60 21 53 ducey-tourisme.com
Avranches 2 rue du Général de Gaulle 02 33 58 00 22
avranches.fr/Tourisme

SNCF
There are several return train options from journey's end back to Paris Montparnasse from Pontorson. Most services use local trains and take around 4 or 5 hours via either Caen, Folligny or Granville. You can also connect with the TGV Atlantique high speed service at Rennes which may be a little quicker, though more expensive and your bike will need its own reserved space made in advance (by contrast bikes can just be wheeled onto many local TER and Corail services).

Since 2013 a special low cost, high-speed service called Ouigo has been operating from Rennes to Paris and stops at Paris Massy TGV station which is near the start of the Limours option of Veloscenic - from there you can cycle back up the Veloscenic greenway towards Paris centre. Bikes must be disassembled and packed in a bag no larger than 90cm x 120cm. **ouigo.com**

Another low cost option is Flixbus, which operates directly between Mont-Saint-Michel and Paris and takes over 5 hours. Again, your bike must be disassembled and bagged. **flixbus.com**

Saint-Léonard

Tombelaine

Ancien Château

Ecomusée de
la Baie
du Mont-Saint-Michel

☆ SEE OVERLEAF

0 Km 1 2

0 Miles 1

Le Mont-
Saint-Michel

Baie du Mont-Sant-Michel

Pointe de
Roche Torin

453.5

4

D 313ᴱ

Le Mont-
Saint-Michel

4

C 201

5

D 288

3

Courtils

1 **2**

La Brasserie
de la Baie

435

D 43

5

6 Céaux

Montitier

German War
Cemetery

9

D 107

7

Mesgnier

D 275

La
Rive

12

445

D 75

10

9 **10**

Ardevon

7 **8**

D 200ᴱ¹

Huisnes

11

ier

440

D 113

8

15

11

13

Tanis

6

Servon

N 175

450

Alligator Bay

12

16

Beauvoir

D 80

Moulin de
Moidrey

Les Pas

14

Brée

D 776

Moidrey

25 **26**

Cycle route
west signed
to Cancale
here

N 175

Curey

27

Pontorson

Base de
Plein Air de
Couesnon
Cycle Hire

Pontorson

D 776

17 **24**

SNCF

Pontorson
Mont/Saint-Michel

D 30

i **Pontorson**
place de l'hôtel de ville
02 33 60 20 65
mont-saint-michel-baie.com
Mont-Saint-Michel
Corps de Garde de Bourgeois
02 33 60 14 30
ot-montsaintmichel.com
There is also a tourist office at
the car park area about a mile
from the Mont itself.

4 D313ᴱ skirts coast past track to Roche Torin
viewpoint.
5 L leaving C201 S Courtils.
6 In Courtils jink L then R by cross, onto D288.
7 At Mesgnier jink L then R onto D133. Bending L out
of Mesgnier, ignore minor R then split R, S Mont-Saint-
Michel.
8 R onto D107 S Montitier.
9 At X-roads L onto D75 S Huisnes.
10 L by German war cemetery, climbing to Huisnes.

11 R in Huisnes at R/B, passing church and descend.
12 L onto D75 S Ardevon and Pontorson.
13 Follow D75 past the edge of Ardevon village,
following signs to Les Pas.
14 R at X-roads in Les Pas onto D80.
15 Meet main road in Beauvoir and jink R then L to
meet tarmac greenway. R is journey's end at Mont-
Saint-Michel and L to Pontorson and Eurovelo 4
cycle route to Cancale.

122

1 MEUBLÉ DE TOURISME H777013 ** /
CHAMBRES D'HÔTES LES BRUYÈRES DU
MONT
5 le Mezeray 50220 Ceaux
02 33 60 08 67 06 58 84 71 51
les-bruyeres-du-mont.fr
B&B and longer term self-catering.

2 CHAMBRES D'HÔTES LA HULOTTE
5 les Forges 50220 Céaux 02 33 68 26 26

3 GÎTES DE FRANCE
CHAMBRES D'HÔTES No G333148
50220 Céaux
02 33 70 96 69 gites-de-france.com

4 CHAMBRES D'HÔTES
LE RAYON DE SOLEIL
14 route de la Baie 50220 Courtils
02 33 60 88 16 lerayondesoleil.monsite-orange.fr

5 CAMPING SAINT-MICHEL ***
35 route du Mont Saint Michel 50220 Courtils
02 33 70 96 90 campingsaintmichel.com
Chalet style holiday homes available as well as
tent pitches (though chalets not available for
single nights in high season).

6 GÎTE DU GRAND MANOIR
3 rue de la Pierre du Tertre 50170 Servon
02 33 68 30 15 gitedugrandmanoir.com
Gîte de groupe accommodating up to 14 – will do
single nights outside of July and August.

7 CHAMBRES D'HÔTES BEL HORIZON
9 rue du Moulin de la Butte 50170 Huisnes-sur- Mer
06 89 24 27 64 / 02 33 70 94 07
chambres-horizon.fr

8 HÔTEL LA CASSEROLE DE LA BAIE
8 rue Grange de Dime 50170 Huisnes-sur- Mer
02 33 60 33 40 lacasseroledelabaie.fr

9 CHEZ MARILYN
19 route de la Baie 50170 Ardevon
06 95 37 27 97

10 PRIEURÉ DU MONT SAINT MICHEL
2 rue du Prieuré 50170 Ardevon
02 33 49 79 72 pelerin-montsaintmichel.org
Tents and dormitories for groups.

11 CAMPING À LA FERME
LA BIDONNIÈRE
5 route de la Rive 50170 Ardevon
06 25 55 30 70
campingcar.ardevivre.fr

12 LES EPINETTES MAISON D'HÔTES
8 bis route du Mont-Saint-Michel
50170 Beauvoir
02 33 68 30 65 les-epinettes-normandie.fr

13 HÔTEL LE BEAUVOIR **
9 route du Mont-Saint-Michel 50170 Beauvoir
02 33 60 09 39 hotel-lebeauvoir.com
Secure bike storage.

14 HÔTEL ROSE
5 route du Mont-Saint-Michel Beauvoir
50170 Mont-Saint-Michel
02 33 60 09 23 hotel-rose.fr

15 CAMPING AUX POMMIERS ****
28 route du Mont-Saint-Michel 50170 Beauvoir
02 33 60 11 36 / 06 20 15 25 14
camping-auxpommiers.com

16 CAMPING GUÉ DE BEAUVOIR *
5 route du Mont-Saint-Michel 50170 Beauvoir
02 33 60 09 23 hotel-gue-de-beauvoir.fr

For accommodation listings **17** to **35** in
Mont-Saint-Michel, Moidrey and Pontorson see
overleaf.

⭐ ROCHE TORIN VIEWPOINT
Short signed detour down a track from the main route. Incredible views across the bay to Mont-Saint-Michel.

⭐ ECOMUSÉE DE LA BAIE DU MONT-SAINT-MICHEL
On the north side of the bay, this musuem has all sorts of displays about the natural history of the area.

⭐ LA BRASSERIE DE LA BAIE
Craft brewery open for visits and sales

⭐ OSSUAIRE ALLEMAND DU MONT D'HUISINES
German war cemetry. An incredible building housing the remains of around 12,000 war dead, with a lookout over Mont-Saint-Michel to the rear.

⭐ ALLIGATOR BAY
The largest collection of alligators in Europe.

⭐ MOULIN DE MOIDREY
Working 1806 windmill. Open daily. Part of the Mont-Saint-Michel World Heritage Site.

⭐ PONTORSON
Popular and attractive base for Mont-Saint-Michel and an attractive town. Église Notre-Dame town dates back to William the Conqueror. Atelier Robert Galgoczi produces stained glass. La Maison Lefranc sells pommeau, cider, calvados etc. The Couesnon Rive Gauche outdoor centre has canoeing, mountain biking and climbing. Good direct bus service right up to Mont-Saint-Michel itself.

⭐ TOMBELAINE - ANCIEN CHÂTEAU
See page 127 for description.

⭐ LE MONT-SAINT-MICHEL
See 'Don't Miss'.

Moulin de Moidrey

Accommodation around Mont-Saint-Michel~Pontorson Greenway

17 BEST WESTERN HÔTEL MONTGOMERY
13 rue Couesnon 50170 Pontorson
02 33 60 00 09 hotel-montgomery.com

18 LOGIS HÔTEL LA TOUR BRETTE
2 rue Couesnon 50170 Pontorson
02 33 60 10 69 latourbrette.fr
Bike storage

19 HÔTEL LE XIV
14 rue du Docteur Tizon 50170 Pontorson
02 33 69 09 29 le-14.com

20 CHAMBRES D'HÔTES ANGEL
5 rue de la Grenouillère 50170 Pontorson
06 11 97 36 87   Bike hire.

21 AU LOGIS DES PINS MAISON D'HÔTES
10 rue de la Grenouillère 50170 Pontorson
09 52 37 57 92 aulogisdespins.fr
Secure bike storage and swimming pool.

22 HÔTEL ARIANE
50 boulevard Clémenceau 50170 Pontorson
02 33 60 03 84 ariane-mt-st-michel.com

23 CENTRE DUGUESCLIN YOUTH HOSTEL
50170 Pontorson 02 33 60 18 65 fuaj.org

24 CAMPING HALIOTIS ***
Chemin des Soupirs 50170 Pontorson
02 33 68 11 59
camping-haliotis-mont-saint-michel.com

25 CHAMBRES D'HÔTES LE RELAIS DE MOIDREY
route de la Grève 50170 Moidrey
02 33 58 70 74 moidrey.com

26 LA BASTIDE DU MOULIN
9 route de la Grève 50170 Moidrey
02 33 58 77 16 labastidedumoulin.fr

27 CHAMBRES D'HÔTES AU PETIT VILLENEUVE
2 route de Villeneuve 50170 Moidrey
02 33 60 85 14 chambremontsaintmichel.fr
Bike storage

28 HÔTEL MERCURE
route du Mont Saint Michel
50170 Le Mont-Saint-Michel
02 33 60 14 18 accorhotels.com

29 HÔTEL VERT
route du Mont Saint Michel
La Caserne 50170 Le Mont-Saint-Michel
02 33 68 40 19 hotels.le-mont-saint-michel.com

30 HÔTEL GABRIEL ***
route du Mont Saint Michel
50170 Le Mont-Saint-Michel
02 33 60 14 13 hotels.le-mont-saint-michel.com

31 CHAMBRES D'HÔTES LA JACOTIÈRE *
La Caserne Ardevon 50170 Le Mont-Saint-Michel
02 33 60 22 94 lajacotiere.fr
Bike storage.

32 HÔTEL LE RELAIS DU ROY
8 route du Mont Saint Michel
50170 Le Mont-Saint-Michel
02 33 60 14 25 hotels.le-mont-saint-michel.com

33 HÔTEL DE LA DIGUE *
La Caserne Ardevon 50170 Le Mont-Saint-Michel
02 33 60 14 02 ladigue.eu

34 LE RELAIS SAINT MICHEL****
La Caserne Ardevon 50170 Le Mont-Saint-Michel
02 33 89 32 00
www.relais-st-michel.fr

35 CAMPING DU MONT SAINT-MICHEL *
route du Mont Saint Michel
50170 Le Mont-Saint-Michel
02 33 60 22 10 camping-montsaintmichel.com

Veloscenic

Mont-Saint-Michel

Fontaine Saint-Aubert

Le Mont Saint-Michel

Chapelle Saint-Aubert

Tour du Nord

Maison et jardin du Curé

Échauguette du Nord

Fontaine Saint-Symphorien

Bastion Tour

Parvis de la Croix de Jérusalem

Knight's House, (Logis Tiphaine)

Le Châtelet

Musée Historique

Église Saint-Pierre

Abbey

Belle Chaise

Musée Archéoscope

Grande Terrasse de l'Ouest

Cimetière

Tour Perrine

Musée de la Mer et de l'Écologie

Logis Abbatiaux

Tour Gabriel

MONTÉE AUX POULAINS

CNIR

Tour de la Liberté

Échauguette de la Pilette

Tour de l'Avancée

Ancienne Hôtellerie de la Sirène

Maison dite de l'Artichaut

Corps de Garde des Bourgeois

Tour de l'Arcade

Mairie du Mont-Saint-Michel

La Mère Poulard

Tour du Roi

PONT-PASSERELLE

Traffic-free path

Pedestrian area / with steps

Footway

Tourist information / Toilets

Viewpoint

Wayside cross / Fountain

Place of Worship / other building

Grass / Heath / Woods

✪ ABBEY

With origins in the 8th century, the current buildings date from the 11th-16th centuries. A unique draw for many thousands from around the world (so it's not suprising there are a number of more modern and commercial attractions on the island too, as listed here). The higher you climb towards the top of the abbey the more staggering are the views across the bay.

✪ LE MUSÉE HISTORIQUE DU MONT-SAINT-MICHEL

Exhibitions covering the 1300 years of Mont-Saint-Michel and the monks who built it.

✪ MUSÉE DE LA MER ET DE L'ÉCOLOGIE

✪ ARCHÉOSCOPE HISTORY SHOW

✪ THE KNIGHT'S HOUSE

Exhibition of the life of a medieval knight.

There are also several companies and people offering guided walks across the bay at low tide, guiding you around the notorious quicksands. They also offer the chance to visit Le Rocher de Tombelaine, a small island with the site of a medieval village and now a nature reserve with access strictly controlled. There is wildlife in abundance including seals and many species of bird. Here's a sample of what is on offer:

Gambettes en Baie Crossings of the bay with a nature guide.   gambettes-enbaie.fr
Virginie Morel French, English and Spanish speaking guide with fun family activities on the bay offered.   virginie-morel.com
Stephane Gueno Guided walks and rides around the bay on a fat bike.   sport-evasion-fr.com
For more guided tours visit:
www.manchetourisme.com/traversee-baie-mont-saint-michel

Another local activity is eating Agneau de pré salé; salt meadow lamb from sheep you can see being grazed on the salt flats around the mount and sold at restaurants throughout the area.

The climb towards the abbey summit.